Good-bye Round Robin

25 Effective Oral Reading Strategies

Updated Edition

Michael F. Opitz
Timothy V. Rasinski

Heinemann
Portsmouth, NH

Heinemann
361 Hanover Street
Portsmouth, NH 03801–3912
www.heinemann.com

Offices and agents throughout the world

Library of Congress Cataloging-in-Publication Data
Opitz, Michael F.
  Good-bye round robin : 25 effective oral reading strategies / Michael F. Opitz, Timothy V. Rasinski. — Updated ed.
      p. cm.
  Includes bibliographical references.
  ISBN-13: 978-0-325-02580-3
  ISBN-10: 0-325-02580-0
  1. Oral reading.   I. Rasinski, Timothy V.   II. Title.

LB1573.5.O65 2008
372.45'2—dc22   2008030934

Editor: Kate Montgomery
Production: Vicki Kasabian
Text design: Joyce Weston Design
Cover design: Night & Day Design
Typesetter: Kim Arney
Manufacturing: Louise Richardson

Printed in the United States of America on acid-free paper
12   RRD   4 5

To all children
who will find joy and satisfaction
through authentic oral reading

Contents

Preface to Updated Edition

S ilent reading is the way we most often read in everyday life. So why is this book about purposeful and meaningful oral reading strategies? And if we are to value *oral* reading, why are we saying good-bye to *round robin reading*, "the outmoded practice of calling on students to read orally one after the other" (Harris and Hodges 1995, 222)?

Answers to these two questions form the foundation of this text. But our desire to round out the answers to these most important questions leads us to emphasize six points in this preface. First, consider the National Reading Panel's findings (2000) on oral reading. As a result of investigating the topic, the panel concluded, "guided repeated oral reading procedures that included guidance from teachers, peers, or parents had a significant and positive impact on word recognition, fluency, and comprehension across a range of levels." They continued, "These results also apply to all students—good readers as well as those experiencing reading difficulties." Given that we want to help children to become the best possible readers, oral reading appears anything but a choice.

But choice *does* enter when we think about the types of oral reading activities we use and why we should use them in place of others. As we emphasize in Chapter 1, there are specific reasons for using oral reading yet there are also numerous reasons for ridding ourselves of *round robin reading*. Clearly, in this text, we say "Hello!" to meaningful, purposeful oral reading strategies and "Good-bye!" to the rest.

Second, we realize that English language learners (ELLs) are the norm rather than the exception in most classrooms, leaving many teachers to search out the best ways to help these children acquire English in authentic contexts. Using specific oral reading strategies shown in this book is one way to do just that. Figure A provides the stages of language proficiencies along with a description of each, implications for oral reading instruction, and specific, appropriate oral reading strategies

Figure A. English Language Proficiency Levels, Descriptions, Implications, and Purposeful Oral Reading Strategies

Stages of Language Proficiency	Description	Implications for Using Oral Reading	Purposeful Oral Reading Strategies
Stage 1: Preproduction (Emerging)	Students are in a silent period in which they listen but do not speak in English. They may respond using nonverbal cues in attempt to communicate basic needs.	Oral reading should be modeled by the teacher and other students. Students in the silent period should not be forced to speak but should be given the opportunity to try, if they want, in a group activity where they won't be singled out.	• Shared Book Experience • Choral Reading • Read-Aloud • Recorded Text • Fast Start (Slight accommodations may need to be made so as not to force production.)
Stage 2: Early Production (Beginning)	Students are beginning to understand more oral language. They respond using one- or two-word phrases and start to produce simple sentences for basic social interactions and to meet basic needs.	Teacher and students should continue to model oral reading. Students should be encouraged to begin taking risks with simple, rehearsed oral reading in non-threatening situations.	• Read to Discover • Shared Book Experience • Choral Reading • Mentor Reading • Paired Reading • Read-Aloud • Recorded Text • Fast Start
Stage 3: Speech Emergence (Developing)	Students' listening comprehension improves, and they can understand written English. Students are fairly comfortable engaging in social conversations using simple sentences, but they are just beginning to develop their academic language proficiency.	Students continue to learn through modeling. Students should be participating in whole-class, small-group, partner, and rehearsed oral reading activities. They will need support and opportunities to practice with feedback before independent or paired oral reading for an audience.	• Think-Aloud • Induced Imagery • Directed Listening Thinking Activity • Revised Radio • Reading • Choral Reading • Mentor Reading • Readers Theatre • Poetry Club • Paired Reading • Listen to Children Read • Fluency Development Lessons • Fast Start

Stages of Language Proficiency	Description	Implications for Using Oral Reading	Purposeful Oral Reading Strategies
Stage 4: Intermediate Fluency (Expanding)	Students understand and frequently use conversational English with relatively high accuracy. They are able to communicate their ideas in both oral and written contexts.	With scaffolding, students can successfully participate in most all oral reading activities that native speakers are expected to complete. Open-ended questions will allow students to demonstrate comprehension and academic language development.	• Think-Aloud • Induced Imagery • Directed Listening Thinking Activity • Look for the Signals • Say It Like the Character • Rapid Retrieval of Information • Revised Radio Reading • Readers Theatre • Read Around • Poetry Club • Read-Aloud • Paired Reading
Stage 5: Advanced Fluency (Bridging)	Students comprehend and engage in conversational and academic English with proficiency. They perform near grade level in reading, writing, and other content areas.	Students should be encouraged to use higher-level thinking skills during their oral reading. They are near native-like proficiency in oral reading, but may still need support with analyzing, inferring, and evaluating.	• Induced Imagery • Directed Listening Thinking Activity • Look for the Signals • Say It Like the Character • Rapid Retrieval of Information • Read-Aloud • Paired Reading • Read Around • Poetry Club

included in this book for each stage. Figure B illustrates how the strategies cut across the various stages. Taken together, both figures serve as reminders that there is much language variation among ELLs. While some oral reading strategies cut across these levels, others are more germane to the distinct stages. Recognizing that there are different stages of language proficiency, teachers can select the most appropriate strategies to maximize students' learning.

Figure B. English Language Proficiency Levels and Oral Reading Strategies

Oral Reading Strategies	Stage 1: Preproduction Silent Period (Entering)	Stage 2: Early Production (Beginning)	Stage 3: Speech Emergence (Developing)	Stage 4: Intermediate Fluency (Expanding)	Stage 5: Advanced Fluency (Bridging)
Think-Aloud	•	•	•	•	•
Induced Imagery		•	•	•	•
Directed Listening Thinking Activity		•	•	•	•
Look for the Signals		•	•	•	•
Say It Like the Character			•	•	•
Rapid Retrieval of Information			•	•	•
Read to Discover				•	•
Revised Radio Reading		•	•	•	
Shared Book Experience	•	•	•		
Choral Reading	•	•	•		
Mentor Reading		•	•	•	
Readers Theater		•	•	•	
Read Around		•	•	•	•
Poetry Club			•	•	•
Read-Aloud	•	•	•	•	•
Paired Reading		•	•	•	•
Recorded Texts	•	•	•		
Listen to Children Read		•	•	•	
Fluency Development Lessons		•	•	•	
Modified Miscue Analysis		•	•	•	•
Retrospective Miscue Analysis		•	•	•	•
Student Self-Evaluation		•	•	•	•
Multidimensional Fluency Scale		•	•	•	•
Reading Rate		•	•	•	•
Fast Start	•	•	•		

Third, there are elementary school teachers who champion oral reading as one way to help children maximize their full potential as readers yet abhor round robin reading, the one and only oral reading strategy they recall from childhood. From them come some valuable insights into the strategies we showcase in this text. Patty comments, "Very often we teachers get stuck in a practice like round robin reading because it is so prevalent. But just because a practice is prevalent doesn't mean it is OK! The strategies in *Good-bye Round Robin* are like little eye-openers, reminding me that reading fluently is an important skill, but there are effective and ineffective ways to best help my students learn it." Julia adds, "The strategies in this book provide authentic read-aloud experiences for students that naturally lead to repeated readings, which strengthens fluency." But perhaps the real clincher comes from Ashley, a first-grade teacher who admonishes, "Throw the popcorn to the robins! It's a new day." What these representative comments help us to see is that more teachers than not are on a quest to discover better ways to instruct the students they are fortunate to teach.

Fourth, with nearly 5,000 children's books published annually, we are not at a loss for fitting authentic books that can assist teachers in teaching the specific oral reading strategies herein. We provide ten titles for each oral reading strategy in this text, each carefully and thoughtfully selected to best coincide with the oral reading strategy. Along with these titles is a new appendix that features more than 100 titles. Taken together, then, we provide approximately 300 of what we consider the best titles to help you teach the oral reading strategies in this text. The majority of these books have 2007–2008 copyright dates.

Fifth, perhaps one of the best ways for children to feel a part of a classroom community is to provide them with opportunities to interact with all students in the class in different grouping configurations. Figure C shows the oral reading strategies in this book and the grouping size you can use for each activity. Some call for more than one group size within a lesson. As you can see, the oral reading strategies lend themselves well to this flexible grouping arrangement.

Figure C. Oral Reading Strategies and Group Sizes

Oral Reading Activities/ Possible Group Sizes	Whole Class	Small Group	Partner	Solo
Developing Comprehension				
• Think-Aloud	•	•	•	•
• Imagery	•	•	•	•
• Directed Listening Thinking Activity	•	•		
• Look for the Signals	•			•
• Say It Like the Character				•
• Rapid Retrieval of Information		•		
• Read to Discover		•	•	•
Sharing and Performing				
• Revised Radio Reading	•	•		
• Shared Book Experience	•			
• Choral Reading	•	•		
• Readers Theatre	•	•		•
• Read Around		•		•
• Poetry Club	•			•
Struggling Reader				
• Read-Aloud	•			
• Paired Reading			•	
• Recorded Texts		•		•
• Fluency Development Lesson	•	•	•	•

Finally, there are several websites that provide some practical ideas for ways to extend the ideas we present in this book. We feature several of these websites in Appendix B. We make no claim that this list is exhaustive. Rather we offer it as a starter list of what we consider to be some of the best sites to assist you in teaching your students.

In 1925, Nila Banton Smith stated, "Our present social needs demand more efficient methods of reading than those which have been employed in the past" (iii). Without question, these words ring true in the new millennium, particularly as they relate to using the purposeful and meaningful oral reading strategies that form the content of this book. We wish to underscore, however, that oral reading supplements and complements silent reading rather than replaces it. Instead of positioning ourselves on an either/or continuum, we suggest using both modes of reading to best help children become avid readers who not only have the skill to read, but the will, too!

Michael F. Opitz

Acknowledgments

We wish to thank all those individuals who have assisted in the updating of this book. First are the many individuals at Heinemann: Leigh Peake, Kate Montgomery, and Maura Sullivan, who suggested the need for this updated version and worked on our behalf to make it happen; Jillian Scahill for tidying up loose ends; Vicki Kasabian for turning the manuscript into the book you see here; Eric Chalek for his writing that appears on the back cover of this book; Joyce Weston for her interior design, and Night and Day Design for the cover design. Our thanks extend to Char Anderson, Patty Carmichael, Ashley Sorenson, Julia Simms, Dana Brungardt, Melissa Burch, Sara Devers, Christy Kocjancic, and the many other teachers who have commented on the book and encouraged us to update it. Finally, we thank two doctoral students at the University of Northern Colorado: Jennifer A. Davis for compiling the children's literature titles and Lindsey M. Guccione for creating Figures A and B that show how English language learners can benefit from the oral reading strategies in this book. To all, we offer our sincere thanks.

I also wish to thank Sheryl, my wife, for her never-ending support and to my university students, who help me keep a fresh perspective by the questions they ask.

Michael F. Opitz

I also wish to thank my wife, Kathy, for the wonderful patience and encouragement she shows her workaholic husband, and my children, Michael, Emily, Mary, and Jennifer, who have helped me learn about the importance of authentic oral reading at home and at school.

Timothy V. Rasinski

Introduction

Teachers are seated, and class begins:

"Good evening everybody! Tonight we'll explore ways to use oral reading in the reading program. Let's begin by reading aloud. Please turn to page 341. John, please begin reading, and the rest of you follow along." John begins to read. As he reads, I [Michael] look around the room to see if everyone is following. I notice that Mary is reading ahead, so I call on her next. Obviously, she doesn't know where to start, so I say, in a disgusted tone, "Mary, I *told* you to follow along. If you had been following, you would know where to start. Go ahead and show her, John." And so the reading continues until all have had their opportunity to read a section "cold." At this point, I instruct them to take out a piece of paper for a comprehension test. I assure them that because they have read the text, they should have no difficulty passing the test.

"Will the score be calculated into our grade for this course?" they ask.

"Certainly," I respond. "If it's important enough for class time, surely it's important enough to consider when looking at your overall performance."

As the teachers reluctantly take out their papers, I can contain myself no longer. "Forget the test," I say. "Let's talk instead about what just happened and how you might have been feeling about it." The classroom erupts as the teachers share their feelings of anxiety and relief. I wait five minutes for the room to return to silence before I invite the class participants to share their individual comments, and more than one eagerly volunteer:

"My hands were sweating."

"My heart started to race, and I had trouble breathing."

"I was trying to figure out your pattern so that I could prepare the part I thought you would have me read."

"The longer I had to wait, the more nervous I became."

"The only thing I could remember was the sense of relief I felt when you called on someone else to read."

"I was *so* embarrassed when you scolded me for not following along and had John show me where to start. I thought about leaving the room."

"When I miscalled a word and you interrupted my reading to correct the word, I felt humiliated. Why, I wondered, were you doing this to me?"

When comments are exhausted, I state, "Many students are expected to do this type of reading nearly every day. Do you think they might have similar feelings?"

Few hold back—their answers come in unison, "Yes!" Some then share how the whole experience brought back unhappy memories of when they were in grade school and how tense they felt when expected to participate in round robin reading—how their main goal was to "save face." Some talk about how they actually got sick to their stomachs in anticipation of their turn, others about how their hands and voices would tremble uncontrollably. After sharing these thoughts, one person continues the discussion by stating that round robin reading shouldn't be used because of the way it makes children feel and that it gives children the wrong idea about reading. "After all," the learner states, "we are seldom asked to read this way in real life. We usually read silently, and when we do read orally before a group, we usually get a chance to rehearse by silently reading ahead of time." Others agree but are quick to justify why they use round robin reading. A close analysis of their responses reveals that their reasons most often reflect classroom management issues. I admire their honesty, thank them for it, and tell them that they appear ready to learn several *effective* oral reading strategies to use in place of round robin reading, defined by Harris and Hodges (1995) as "the outmoded practice of calling on students to read orally one after the other" (222).

As this scenario suggests, although round robin reading is "outmoded," it is often used without examining the rationale for its use or the exploration for more effective alternatives. As Allington (1984) noted more than twenty years ago, "oral reading is a form of assessment or practice but often without a clearly developed, or delivered, instructional focus" (834). Is oral reading important? Absolutely! In fact, it is so important that we must put it into perspective and use it in the most effective and efficient ways possible.

We have written this book to help teachers do just that. Our aim is to share several effective and efficient ways to use oral reading and to show where oral reading fits into the reading program. Our primary goal is to provide you—novice and veteran teacher alike—with effective oral reading strategies that you can use to best teach all children to read. The book comprises research-based, practical, kid-tested ways to use oral reading to help all students develop comprehension, share information, and discover effective reading strategies. We also provide techniques for helping struggling readers, as well as ideas for involving parents.

To begin, you'll examine our definition of reading and our reasons for advocating oral reading. Yes—silent reading is used most often in everyday life, and it should remain the mainstay of any effective reading program. However, there are times when oral reading is needed, too. Consider, for example when oral reading is used in response to a request (e.g., "Look in the television guide and tell me what's on at 9:00.") or when ordering from a menu in a restaurant. Then, too, there are those who share a poem on Poet's Night at the local bookstore or coffee house. And how about the many times that we, as parents, are called upon to read aloud to our children? Clearly, children need both types of reading experiences to become strategic readers—readers who use linguistic cues (i.e., semantic, syntactic, and graphophonic), pragmatics (i.e., the context in which the reading is happening and the type of text that is being read), and cognitive cues (i.e., predicting, confirming, self-correcting when meaning is disrupted)—to ensure that comprehension occurs. Indeed, strategic readers are those who can and do use these cues to read all types of reading material, both orally and silently, for a variety of purposes—enjoyment, finding or sharing specific information, completing their work—in their everyday lives.

Chapter 1 provides an overview of the effective oral reading strategies explained in this book. Each is designed to help students learn specific reading strategies, which leads to more skillful reading. Chapter 2 provides ways to use oral reading to enhance comprehension ability, and Chapter 3 presents numerous ways to use oral reading for sharing and performing. Chapter 4 offers several suggestions for using oral reading to help children who find learning to read difficult. We offer a list of *suggested children's books* for each activity in each of these chapters. You will undoubtedly have your own favorites to add to these starter lists. *Teacher Voices* also accompany each oral reading strategy to show how teachers actually use the strategy in their classrooms. Finally, an *Extensions/Tips/Connections* section provides additional ways to use the strategy and additional teaching techniques.

Using oral reading to assess reading is important because it reveals the specific strategies children use, as well as those that require further development. As with any assessment strategy, however, both teachers and students need to understand why and what it is that we are trying to assess. Chapter 5 addresses these issues and provides several appropriate assessment techniques.

Many times, parents want suggestions for how to best help their children with reading. They also want reassurance that what they are doing is "right." Chapter 6 provides support for parents. We offer effective guidelines for reading aloud, along with specific references that parents can use to find good books to read to their children. Finally, in Chapter 7, we attempt to answer the most common questions about oral reading.

We invite you to try the techniques provided in this volume as you see fit and at your own pace. All learning entails risk. Take learning to swim, for example; some individuals dive head first into a swimming pool, totally immersing their bodies in the water all at once. Others gradually enter the pool, slipping in one toe at a time. Attempting new teaching strategies is much the same. We encourage you to celebrate your successes, persist, and keep in mind that children are always worth our best efforts.

CHAPTER 1

Understanding Reading

*S*ilent reading is the key to effective reading. Not surprisingly, then, the reading we encourage in our classrooms should be silent as well. In this way, our students' in-school reading will match the reading we typically do outside of school, which is nearly always silent. Silent reading is faster and provides individuals time to reread without burdening other readers. In fact, Ian Wilkinson (Armbruster and Wilkinson 1991) discovered that when compared with oral reading, group silent reading enabled students to be more attentive during reading and more responsive during discussions following the reading; that is, they could more easily recall information from the text and locate specific information from the text to support answers.

So why do we recommend oral reading yet caution against the all-too familiar round robin reading? In this chapter, we address this question and provide a framework for effective reading instruction for all children. Let's begin with our definition of reading. It provides the foundation for the effective oral reading strategies we explain in this book.

So What Is Reading, Anyhow?

A variety of models have been created to answer this most important question, and about the only two attributes they share in common are a theorist who argues for each and an agreement that comprehension is the essence of reading (Ruddell, Ruddell, and Singer 1994). These different models remind us that reading is a complex, multidimensional process in which readers bring their own meaning and experiences to the printed page to obtain meaning from it. Indeed, our definition of reading is informed by these models. But our own experiences as readers and as teachers, working with children, have also informed our three-part definition:

1. **Reading is language.** When reading, readers use three linguistic cueing systems, which they know intuitively: semantic, syntactic, and graphophonic. They derive semantic cues from the text's meaning, syntactic cues from the text's grammatical structure, and graphophonic cues from sound-letter relationships and patterns. All three of these cueing systems are important and are constantly in motion to enable readers to construct meaning (Figure 1–1). They help readers answer questions such as, "Does this make sense? Does this sound right? Does this look right?"

2. **Reading is a cognitive process.** Readers predict what they think the text is about to convey, sample words or letters within words, and confirm their predictions by checking to see if meaning is maintained. Indeed, readers monitor their reading to ensure understand-

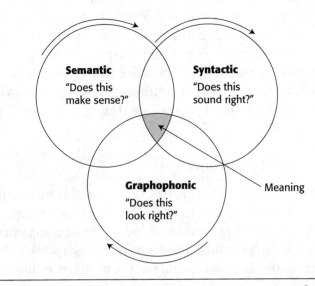

Figure 1–1. *Three Linguistic Cueing Systems: Semantic, Syntactic, and Graphophonic*

ing and take corrective action when meaning breaks down. For example, they may choose to self-correct or continue to read ahead, only to return later to recoup the meaning from the text they initially failed to understand. In other words, readers are strategic. They use a variety of strategies to ensure comprehension.

3. **Reading is a social activity.** Readers use pragmatics—the context in which they are reading (e.g., school, bed, the doctor's office) and the type of book they are reading (e.g., textbook, novel, magazine)—to help guide their reading. They choose to read one type of book while sitting in an overstuffed chair and another while sitting at a desk, depending on their purpose for reading. Clearly, reading serves multiple purposes in our daily lives. We use it to share information and to learn from one another. We use it to learn more about ourselves and to complete specific activities such as hobbies and job-related tasks. We use it to enrich our lives—for pure enjoyment!

Twelve Reasons for Using Oral Reading

Our definition of *reading* undergirds effective use of oral reading. Reading is language and, as such, has a social dimension. Oral reading is necessary when we want to share information with another individual (e.g., "Would you listen to this and tell me how it sounds?"). It is also needed when we, as teachers, are trying to determine whether a child is using language cues effectively. Following are twelve specific reasons to use oral reading within the total reading program. You may well think of others to add to our list.

1. **To whet students' appetites for reading.** By reading books aloud, teachers fill students' heads with the beauty and rhythm of language, introducing children to the rich and varied possibilities of language. This is also an excellent way to expose children to a wide variety of reading materials, such as books, newspaper articles of interest, favorite poems, and perhaps even pieces of their own writing. Sharing this variety, teachers show students what it means to live a full, literate life. Students learn that reading is a part of life and is useful for a variety of reasons, including simple enjoyment. Teachers can

also model for students how to read different types of writing. For example, as he reads a factual article, the teacher can show how it helps to stop occasionally to mentally summarize key information. The teacher can, in another instance, demonstrate skimming—how to find specific information quickly. And, of course, as the teacher reads beautiful literature, such as Gardiner's *Stone Fox*, aloud, his voice can reveal the power of an author's words—words that invite both reflection and tears. As Freire (1985) reminds us, "Reading is not dancing on top of words. It is grasping the soul of them."

2. **To share or perform.** Oral reading is a way for everyone to share information. Sometimes the sharing is informal (e.g., "Hey! Listen to this!"); at other times it is more formal (e.g., "I would like to read you information I discovered on page 37"). On other occasions, oral reading is an integral part of a performance. For example, students may participate in a dramatic play or recite a poem. Again, through this sharing, students see the value of reading and the pleasure it can bring. They also see that reading written language aloud is a way of communicating with others "the ideas, information, feeling, mood, or action that is in printed or written form" (Artley 1972, 47). Chapter 3 provides a wealth of ways to invite students to share and perform.

3. **To help beginning readers better understand how speaking is related to the other language arts and to their lives.** As a result of reading text aloud, students begin to see that what can be written can also be read aloud. They begin to understand that writing, reading, and speaking are all related language processes. They also begin to understand that reading and listening are integral to everyday life, both in and out of school. In Donald Graves' words (1983), "To be literate is to listen, observe intently, see what the moment gives and ask, 'what does it mean?'"

4. **To develop listening comprehension and vocabulary.** As students listen to others read aloud, they expand their listening vocabularies. Research suggests that children increase their vocabularies by merely listening to stories read aloud, even without teacher explana-

tion of word meanings (Elley 1989). An expanded listening vocabulary assists reading growth by providing readers with the sounds and meanings of words that can be read. Identifying a familiar word is much easier and more likely than if the word is foreign to the ear. Listening also helps reading by providing the reader with models of what written language sounds like. Having a sense of these language structures provides readers with an understanding of what they can expect to see when reading. As Huey (1908 [1968]) noted years ago, "The ear and not the eye is the nearest gateway to the child-soul . . ." (334).

5. **To assist students in developing numerous skills associated with reading.** Students should be able to read with fluency, expression, and correct phrasing—all indicators of effective, meaningful reading. Research has shown that oral reading is one of the best ways to help children develop these skills, as well as the many others shown in Figure 1–2 (Reutzel, Hollingsworth, and Eldredge 1994). Chapter 2 provides several activities that help students develop these most important skills.

6. **To promote language learning for students whose first language is not English.** McCauley and McCauley (1992) cite four factors that are important for acquisition of a second language: a low-anxiety environment, repeated practice, comprehensible input, and drama. A low-anxiety environment is one in which trust and respect reign; learners feel free to take risks. Repeated practice provides students with the time and repetition necessary to improve fluency. Comprehensible input enables the learner to understand what is being said. The sensitive teacher deliberately uses language that the learner knows along with language that is unknown. Doing so ensures comprehension and growth. Drama enables the learner to use language in a social setting. It can help the learner make connections between speech and action. All of these factors are addressed when oral reading—Choral Reading in particular—is used, and they provide enough support to enable English language learners, regardless of stage (see Figures A and B in the preface), to read with relative ease.

	Developing Comprehension							Sharing and Performing						
	Think-Aloud	Induced Imagery	Directed Listening Thinking Activity	Look for the Signals	Say It Like the Character	Rapid Retrieval of Information	Read to Discover	Revised Radio Reading	Shared Book Experience	Choral Reading	Mentor Reading	Readers Theatre	Read Around	Poetry Club
Positive attitudes/ Interest in reading	•	•	•	•	•	•	•	•	•	•	•	•	•	•
Reading comprehension	•	•		•	•	•	•	•	•	•	•	•	•	•
Listening comprehension	•	•	•					•	•			•		•
Vocabulary	•		•	•	•	•	•	•	•	•	•	•	•	•
Use of language cues			•	•	•	•	•	•	•	•	•	•	•	•
Predicting	•	•	•	•					•		•	•		
Forming images	•	•	•						•	•	•	•		•
Using prior knowledge	•	•		•	•	•	•	•	•	•	•	•	•	•
Monitoring	•					•		•			•	•		•
Inferring	•	•	•	•	•		•	•	•	•	•	•		•
Expression (fluency)			•	•	•	•	•	•	•	•	•	•	•	•
Phrasing (fluency)			•	•	•	•		•	•	•	•	•	•	•
Skimming			•		•	•							•	

Figure 1–2. *Effective Oral Reading Strategies and Skills They Help Develop*

	Struggling Readers					Guiding Assessment					Home
	Read-Aloud	Paired Reading	Recorded Texts	Listen to Children Read	Fluency Development Lesson	Modified Miscue Analysis	Retrospective Miscue Analysis	Student Self-Evaluation	Multidimensional Fluency Scale	Reading Rate	Fast Start
	•	•	•	•	•		•	•		•	•
		•	•	•	•	•	•	•	•	•	•
	•	•	•		•						•
	•	•	•	•	•	•			•		•
		•	•		•	•	•		•		•
	•	•	•		•						•
	•	•	•		•						
		•			•						
		•		•	•	•	•		•		
		•	•	•							
	•	•	•	•	•			•	•		
		•	•	•	•		•	•			

7. **To build confidence.** As students repeatedly rehearse a selection to read aloud, they grow in their confidence and ability to perform in front of others. The added practice provides time for them to work through any problem areas so that when they are sharing, they read with ease and are able to focus on expressing the meaning the words should convey. They experience firsthand that they can communicate with an interested audience and that they have no reason to feel afraid to share with others.

8. **To further develop comprehension.** Authors not only use specific language to convey their thoughts, but they also use typographical cues such as punctuation marks, bold print, italics, and different sizes of print to signal intended meaning. We want students to pay attention to both so that they can better comprehend the authors' intended meaning. Chapter 2 provides ideas for helping students learn to use these cues—what they are and how they aid comprehension.

9. **To determine the strategies used when reading.** Oral reading is often used as a window into how children read on their own (Goodman 1965, 1996). As children read, teachers listen, observe, and take notes to determine which strategies the child uses and those that need further development. Students, too, can use the results of their oral reading to better understand how they read. For example, when teachers record exactly how a student reads a text and then gives this assessment data to the child, the child, with teacher guidance, can reflect on the strategies she used and those she needs to develop further. Likewise, when students are invited to listen to a taped recording of their own reading, they can hear firsthand if their reading sounds like language we use in everyday life. If they are provided with some sort of checklist of the specific attributes of effective reading (see page 95), they can use it to validate what they are doing, as well as determine what needs improvement. Chapter 5 lists assessment techniques that can be used for this purpose.

ding progress with self and
mpetent readers, they can
lves, to their parents, and to
oud to them or taping their
s a performance assessment
tudents to read periodically
m to see their own growth.
st and last recordings of the
ting students to do so also
ess that happens over time
is the result.

ading time necessary for
hown that children's read-
nber of hours they spend
1988; Postlethwaite and
ig and performing is one
ldren with the additional
ing. As children rehearse
instance, they are pro-
 gful reading. When they
oem that they want to
ing practice occurs. To
read!

arts standards. Stan-
guage arts standards
lls for students to use
ge in different ways so that they can communicate
with many different audiences and for a variety of purposes. The
many different oral reading activities in this volume can fulfill this
standard with ease. The Poetry Club offers one type of reading and
audience, whereas Paired Reading provides another. Reading aloud
for assessment offers yet another way that oral reading is used to
communicate to a specific audience.

Why Move Away from Round Robin Reading?

Round robin reading—defined in *The Literacy Dictionary* as "the out-moded practice of calling on students to read orally one after the other" (Harris and Hodges 1995, 222)—poses many problems:

1. **It provides students with an inaccurate view of reading.** In everyday life, we are rarely expected to read aloud before a group before we have prepared. When we do read aloud before a group, we most often expect others to listen to the information we want to share rather than expect them to follow along. In fact, when we read aloud, the audience often does not have a copy of what we are reading. Likewise, when reading every single word with accuracy becomes the goal for every single lesson, students develop the notion that all reading must be word-perfect, clearly a misconception. If we want to provide children with a realistic view of reading, we need to ensure that the activities we ask them to complete are like those that readers actually do.

2. **It can potentially cause faulty reading habits instead of effective reading strategies.** Students tend to read at different rates, their eyes making stops across the page, stops in which they focus on three or four words. If a student is expected to follow along while another reads, and the reader absorbs only two or three words at each stop, repeats them several times, and identifies so few words that meaning is lost, those who are following along may also develop these habits and short-circuit their growth toward proficient reading. Furthermore, they may come to associate frustration and nonsense with reading—an unfortunate development, indeed.

3. **It can cause unnecessary subvocalization.** While one reader is reading aloud, the others are expected to follow along, reading silently. Because oral reading is slower than silent reading, the silent readers are therefore encouraged to subvocalize every word. This subvocalization may become internalized and cause slower reading rates.

4. **It can cause inattentive behaviors, leading to discipline problems.** Although students are expected to follow along, they rarely do. Instead, they are reading ahead, because either they are faster read-

ers than the person who is reading aloud or they are practicing the part they will be expected to read. Or they aren't paying attention at all but are poking and whispering to the other children. The result? Little attention is given to the meaning of the passage being read. Also, some children may be reprimanded for not following along, which leads them to a less than favorable view of reading.

5. **It can work against all students developing to their full potential.** Research has shown that when children make a mistake when reading aloud—especially children who are struggling with reading—they are corrected by others before they have an opportunity to correct themselves (Allington 1980). One of the most important skills for *all* children to learn, however, is to monitor themselves, paying attention to meaning and self-correcting when meaning is interrupted. Because less proficient readers are generally not afforded this opportunity, they are less likely to develop this most important skill.

6. **It consumes valuable classroom time that could be spent on other meaningful activities.** Because oral reading, being much slower than silent reading, takes longer, the number of words that students will read over a school year can actually decrease (Stanovich 1986). Add to this slower rate the additional time that is used to keep students on track, reminding them where to focus, and a considerable amount of time has been invested in an ineffective activity.

7. **It can be a source of anxiety and embarrassment for students.** As the teacher comments in the introduction to this book reveal, reading aloud to others without an opportunity to rehearse causes much anxiety and embarrassment. Students are so focused on "saving face" that they forget the real purpose of reading—to comprehend. A colleague's son says it best: "You know, Mom, every time Matt has to read aloud, he starts crying. Why does the teacher make him do it?"

8. **It can hamper listening comprehension.** Instead of truly listening to others read, students are preoccupied with following lines of print and looking ahead, either because they are bored or because they are trying to give themselves some practice before they will be expected to read aloud before others. In short, they are distracted.

Yet we know that listening is an important skill. Some studies suggest that listening comprehension and reading comprehension are related and that children who do poorly with listening comprehension will also do poorly with reading comprehension (see Daneman 1991 for a review of these studies). As Sloan and Lotham (1981) comment, "In terms of listening and meaning-making, this strategy is a disaster" (135).

Clearly, although oral reading can be beneficial, round robin reading is not. It more often prohibits rather than facilitates the ability to read. And, as Savage (1998) notes, "It fails to meet the legitimate purposes of reading aloud" (330). Fortunately, there are some excellent alternatives. Figure 1–2 shows these alternatives—effective oral reading strategies—and the specific reading skills and strategies that each will help students develop. When reviewing these strategies, three reminders are in order:

1. First and foremost, students need opportunities to silently read their texts. Doing so better ensures that all students are engaged with the reading. Silent reading has also been more positively related to reading achievement than has small-group oral reading (Allington 1984). This should not come as a surprise when we remember that silent reading is faster. When reading silently, the eye can move much more quickly, taking in more information than when reading orally and having to slow down to enunciate every word. Thus, reading silently enables more reading of connected text, which is meaningful practice, indeed.

2. There is a place for oral reading in the classroom in addition to silent reading, but it must be done for specific, authentic purposes: to develop comprehension, to share information, to determine strategies students use in reading, and to help a struggling reader achieve greater fluency. Oral reading is a means to an end, not the end itself.

3. Figure 1–2 (pp. 6–7) is meant to show the many skills that the oral reading strategies help children develop. It is designed to provide an overview rather than a discrete listing of individual skills to be "drilled and killed."

CHAPTER 2

Developing Comprehension

Comprehension—the essence of reading—is a complex process. "Good" comprehenders are those who demonstrate an understanding of this complexity by using a variety of strategies when reading. These strategies include determining which information is most important, self-questioning, summarizing, inferring, predicting, interpreting, and imaging (Dole, Duffy, Roehler, and Pearson 1991; Pressley, El-Dinary, Gaskins, Schuder, Bergman, Almasi, and Brown 1992; Long, Winograd, and Bridge 1989). More often than not, however, we need to teach children how to use these comprehension strategies as well as how specific typographical signals such as punctuation marks, italics, and boldface type help to convey the author's intended message.

We can use oral reading to teach these strategies. When using a Think-Aloud (see page 15), for example, we can show students how an experienced reader sometimes stops and questions what is being read to make sure that comprehension is occurring. The Think-Aloud can also be used to show readers how background knowledge can help us understand a text; that is, we bring meaning to the page to get meaning from it. Using Look for the Signals (see page 28) can show children how different markings on a page can affect just how they read—what to emphasize, where to pause, where to stop—enabling them to interpret the author's intended meaning. Ultimately, then, we want students to understand that, in addition to their own related experiences, they need to pay attention to both the "deep level" (the author's intended message conveyed by characteristics such as character and plot development) and the "surface level" (those markings that the reader can actually see) to obtain meaning from text.

As Figure 2–1 illustrates, the oral reading strategies in this chapter not only help children develop comprehension, but also help students develop other attributes associated with skillful readers—phrasing and skimming, to name but two.

	Effective Oral Reading Strategies						
Reading Skills/Strategies	Think-Aloud	Induced Imagery	Directed Listening Thinking Activity	Look for the Signals	Say It Like the Character	Rapid Retrieval of Information	Read to Discover
Positive attitudes/Interest in reading	•	•	•	•	•	•	•
Reading comprehension	•	•	•	•	•	•	•
Listening comprehension	•	•	•				
Vocabulary	•		•	•	•	•	•
Use of language cueing systems				•	•	•	•
Predicting	•	•	•	•			
Forming images	•	•					
Using prior knowledge	•	•			•	•	•
Monitoring	•					•	
Inferring	•	•	•	•	•		•
Expression (fluency)					•	•	•
Phrasing (fluency)					•	•	•
Skimming					•		•

Figure 2–1. *Effective Oral Reading Strategies and Skills for Developing Comprehension*

Think-Aloud

Grade Levels: K–5

Description

Much research has revealed that students who have difficulty comprehending often fail to realize that the purpose of reading is to understand a message (Johns 1984, 1986; Opitz 1989). The *Think-Aloud* is one of the best ways to help them see that reading is about comprehending and that readers can and do use a variety of strategies to overcome hurdles that interfere with meaning. During a Think-Aloud, the teacher verbalizes her thoughts while reading aloud, which shows students what experienced readers actually do to ensure comprehension. Davey (1983) lists five strategies that poor comprehenders appear to lack: predicting, forming mental images while reading, using what they already know about the topic (prior knowledge), monitoring how well they are comprehending during reading, and fixing problems as they occur when reading. You can highlight these strategies during the Think-Aloud.

Teaching Suggestions (based on Davey 1983)

1. Select a passage to read aloud. The passage should have points that will pose some difficulties, such as ambiguity and unknown words.
2. Begin reading the passage aloud while students follow along. When you come to a trouble spot, stop and think through it aloud while students listen to what you have to offer.
3. Once you have completed reading orally, invite students to add their thoughts to yours.
4. Pair up students and have them practice the procedure with one another. Each can take turns reading and responding to the other.
5. Have students use the procedure when they are reading silently. Readers could use a form such as Figure 2–2 to remind themselves of what they need to be doing to ensure comprehension and to evaluate themselves.

How Did I Do When Reading?

Name _____ Date _____

Title of selection _____

	never	sometimes	a lot
1. I made predictions.	_____	_____	_____
2. I was able to form a picture in my mind.	_____	_____	_____
3. I made connections.	_____	_____	_____
4. I knew when I was having problems.	_____	_____	_____
5. I did something to fix my problems.	_____	_____	_____

Figure 2–2. *How Did I Do When Reading?*

© 2008 Michael F. Opitz and Timothy V. Rasinski, from *Good-bye Round Robin: 25 Effective Oral Reading Strategies, Updated Edition*. Portsmouth, NH: Heinemann.

Suggested Titles

Title	Author (Last, First)	Publisher/Year ISBN	Suggested Grade Levels
Copper Sun	Draper, Sharon M.	Simon Pulse/2006 9781416953487	6–8
The Birthday Tree	Fleischman, Paul	Candlewick/2008 9780763626044	2–4
Oh, Brother!	Grimes, Nikki	Greenwillow/2008 9780688172954	K–5
A Sweet Smell of Roses	Johnson, Angela	Aladdin/2005 9781416953616	2–5
The Jupiter Stone	Lewis, Paul O.	Tricycle/2003 1582461074	1–4
The Mozart Question	Morpurgo, Michael	Candlewick/2006 9780763635527	4–8
Colors of Mexico	Olawsky, Lynn A.	First Avenue Editions/1997 1575052164	2–3
Tulip Sees America	Rylant, Cynthia	Scholastic/2002 0439399785	1–2
I Love My Hair	Tarpley, Natasha	Little, Brown/2003 0316525588	2
Old Turtle and the Broken Truth	Wood, Douglas	Scholastic/2003 0439321093	3–6

Teacher Voices

To demonstrate the Think-Aloud procedure to his fourth graders, Michael used a legend from *Eagle Walking Turtle's Full Moon Stories: Thirteen Native American Legends* (1997). Because the class was reading legends, he felt that the demonstration would better help students apply what they had learned to their actual reading experiences. After looking at the cover, he commented, "Just from reading this title, I can tell that this is going to be a book filled with legends. In fact, the author even tells me that there will be thirteen legends in this book." He then stated, "I already know something about legends. Legends are stories that state traditions and beliefs of a given group of people. I'll bet that these stories will be about some of the traditions and beliefs of Native American people." He then provided students with a copy of "The Magpie," the first legend in the book and the one that he would use for the remainder of his Think-Aloud. He began reading aloud as the students followed along. He read the first two paragraphs, stopped, and commented, "I'm getting a picture of the house where the story is told. It is made of logs and it has a wood stove to keep everyone warm." He then read the next paragraph and once again stopped and commented, "This reminds me of how my cousin used to tell me stories. Instead of sitting in a circle on the floor, though, we sat on the bed." He read the next paragraph, stopped, and commented, "Wow! I am surprised that the Thunder-beings would think that the people were not worth saving. I expected them to believe this already." He then continued reading and stopped after reading the word *astonished*, at which point he stated, "'Astonished.' Hmm. I wonder what that means. This is a new word for me. I better read that sentence again and see if the other words can help me figure out what it means."

A close analysis of this scenario reveals that Michael focused on several strategies that poor comprehenders often need to be taught to use. The first comment helps students to see how an experienced reader *makes predictions*, whereas the second shows students how a reader *uses prior knowledge* to make connections with new reading material. The third shows that good readers *form visual images* when they read. The fourth comment once again shows how a reader uses *prior knowledge* to make connections with the reading. The last two comments demonstrate *monitoring* one's comprehension and *fixing* a part that interferes with meaning.

Extensions/Tips/Connections

- While several strategies were modeled in Michael's Think-Aloud, keep in mind that not all need to be present in all Think-Aloud sessions. In fact, you may want to focus on one or two of the strategies to better help students use them when reading on their own—the ultimate goal of this instruction.

• *Reverse Think-Alouds* (Block 1997) add some variety and can help you determine whether students are internalizing the specific strategies they need to use when reading. With this procedure, students ask you what you are thinking rather than being told. You ask the student(s) to follow along silently while you read orally and to stop you during your reading to ask questions about what you are thinking at a given time. These questions can focus on how you figured out a given word, clarify what the author is trying to say, or summarize a given section. The types of questions that students ask can reveal which strategies they are focusing on and which need to be developed further.

Induced Imagery

Grade Levels: 1–8

Description

Research has revealed that the ability to form mental images is an effective reading strategy. That is, readers who are able to use imagery to aid their understanding and remembering show enhanced reading comprehension performance (Gambrell and Jawitz 1993). In addition to helping students remember, creating mental images also enhances readers' abilities to construct inferences and make predictions. *Induced Imagery* is one way to teach students how to construct mental images. First, the teacher models how to construct an image, then guides the students as they construct their own images, and finally provides students with independent practice.

Teaching Suggestions (based on Gambrell, Kapinus, and Wilson 1987)

1. Select a passage to read aloud. The passage should contain much description so that students are better able to see how words can help to form mental pictures, and it should be brief (about 100 words). Make an overhead transparency of the passage or print it on a chart large enough for all to see.
2. Model the entire procedure for the students, focusing on *what* you are doing, *why* mental imagery is of value, and *how* to actually do it.
3. Provide students with guided practice. To begin, read the first part of another prepared passage. Read aloud the first part and tell them the images you are forming. Then invite students to tell about their images. They can also note likes and differences among the images.
4. Either pair or group students and give one member a passage to read silently. After this individual has had time to prepare, ask him to read it aloud to the others in the group and to talk about the mental images he is forming. Invite other students in the group to share their images and to explain what caused them to form the particular image.

5. Provide students with time to apply mental imagery independently while reading their self-selected books. You might want to have students draw one of their mental images, noting the corresponding page(s) in their books. These could be shared with others or serve as a performance assessment of how well they are able to use mental imagery.

Suggested Titles

Title	Author (Last, First)	Publisher/Year ISBN	Suggested Grade Levels
James and the Giant Peach	Dahl, Roald	Penguin/1996 9780140374247	3–5
The Honey Makers	Gibbons, Gail	HarperCollins/1997 0688175317	1–3
Healing Water: A Hawaiian Story	Hostetter, Joyce	Calkins Creek/2008 9781590785140	5–8
Wind Flyers	Johnson, Angela	Simon & Schuster/2007 9780689848797	1–4
When the Fireflies Come	London, Jonathan	Dutton/2003 0525454047	K–3
How Mama Brought the Spring	Manushkin, Fran	Dutton/2008 9780525420279	K–3
The Sound of Day, The Sound of Night	O'Neil, Mary	Melanie Kroupa/2003 0374371350	K–2
Maple Syrup Season	Purmell, Ann	Holiday House/2008 9780823418916	K–3
Maniac Magee	Spinelli, Jerry	Ashton Scholastic/1992 0316807222	4–8
Mary Ingalls on Her Own	Willard, Elizabeth Kimmel	HarperCollins/2008 9780060009069	3–7

Teacher Voices

Connie's fifth-grade class was beginning to read *Dear Mr. Henshaw* (Cleary 1983). She decided that this would be a good novel to use to teach mental imagery because many of the letters are descriptive. She also wanted her students to see how they could apply this strategy to an authentic text. Following the foregoing suggestions, she said something like this:

> Today I am going to share a strategy that can help you remember what you have read. It's called mental imagery. Mental imagery is a process of making pictures in our minds of different parts of the book—characters, events, how something looks—to help us better understand what we're reading. First I'll show you how I do it, and then I'll give you some practice. While I am reading the passage, 1 will tell you how I am using mental imagery to understand and remember.

She proceeded to read the first paragraph of the first letter, which she had copied from *Dear Mr. Henshaw* onto an overhead transparency. As she read, she said the following,

> This is a letter. I can imagine a boy sitting at a table writing a letter. I usually write my letters at my kitchen table. I can also see the boy holding his pencil and writing on a piece of lined notebook paper. He's telling Mr. Henshaw about a book he read, and he's giving me a good idea about the size of the book. He says it's thick with chapters. I can see that book. It reminds me of my first thick book. I can see him being happy with himself for finishing the book and can sense his feeling of accomplishment. That's how I felt when I finished my first thick chapter book. My picture includes a boy sitting at a kitchen table all by himself. For some reason, I feel like the boy is lonely—maybe being alone as he writes this letter makes me think so.

She then read the second paragraph of the letter, but this time she invited the students to share their images and how they arrived at those images. Finally, she paired students to provide some practice with imagery. One student read the letter shown on page 3 and the other read the letter on page 4. Once each had rehearsed their letter by reading it silently, each read it aloud to their partner and talked about the mental images that they were forming and why.

She concluded by saying, "Mental images can help us to both understand and remember. You can use them when reading all kinds of books. Today we tried them with a story. We'll be trying them again with other types of books."

Extensions/Tips/Connections

Jane Fowler and Stephanie Newlon (1995) suggest using paper cameras to help students "zoom in" on a given part of a story. They provide an outline of a camera and direct students to draw, on the back of it, a picture of one story component, such as a character, the setting, or an event. They then suggest stringing a piece of yarn through each camera so that students can wear them and share their pictures with others.

Directed Listening
Thinking Activity (DLTA)

Grade Levels: K–8

Description

As stated in Chapter 1, an expanded listening vocabulary assists reading growth by providing readers with the sounds and meanings of words that can be read. Indeed, identifying a familiar word is much easier and more likely than if the word is foreign to the ear. Listening also helps reading by providing the reader with models of what written language sounds like. The *DLTA* is one way that the teacher can help prepare children for independent reading. Using this strategy, the teacher reads aloud, stopping at appropriate points along the way to engage students in an ongoing discussion.

Teaching Suggestions (based on Gillet and Temple 1994)

1. Preview the text to be read to the students.

2. Relate the selection to the students' lives by discussing possible topics that may be addressed in the selection and their knowledge about these topics. Also invite them to make predictions based on the title.

3. Read the text aloud as the students listen. Stop at designated points to confirm or change predictions and to make new questions and predictions for the next section of the text.

4. Read to the next logical stopping point and, again, confirm, discuss, question, and make new predictions.

5. When you are finished, ask students to summarize the selection. You may also wish to have students devise some questions that could be used in future readings of the text.

Suggested Titles

Title	Author (Last, First)	Publisher/Year ISBN	Suggested Grade Levels
I'll Never Share You, Blackboard Bear	Alexander, Martha	Candlewick/2003 0763615900	K–1
Woof! Woof!	Carter, David A.	Little Simon/2006 1415665567	K–5
When Harriet Met Sojourner	Clinton, Catherine	Amistad/2007 9780060504250	2–5
Free Baseball	Corbett, Sue	Puffin/2006 978052547202	3–8
Lightship	Floca, Brian	Atheneum/2007 9781416924364	K–3
Kids at Work	Freedman, Russell	Clarion/1994 0395797268	4–6
Click! A Book About Cameras and Taking Pictures	Gibbons, Gail	Little, Brown/1997 0316309761	2–4
Pitching in for Eubie	Nolen, Jerdine	Amistad/2007 9780688149178	1–3
The Mysterious Case of the Allbright Academy	Stanley, Diane	HarperCollins/2008 9780060858186	3–7
Jackalope	Stevens, Janet	Harcourt/2003 0152167366	1–4

Teacher Voices

Shauna used Elizabeth O'Donnell's *Maggie Doesn't Want to Move* (1987) when constructing a DLTA for her second-grade class. She decided to use this book because it would provide students with an opportunity to use higher-level comprehension to discover unstated characteristics of characters—they would need to "read between the lines." Using the foregoing suggestions, she said the following:

> I would like for all of you to close your eyes and think back to your first day of class this year. Think about the types of feelings you had. Think about the fears of entering a new classroom.

After inviting students to share their thoughts, she continued,

> Today I am going to read the story *Maggie Doesn't Want to Move*. Because this is our first time through the story, I will stop a few times and ask you to make some predictions. I will also ask you some questions about Maggie and Simon, her older brother.

She then began reading the story. She stopped on page 4 and asked, "What can you tell about Maggie so far? How many think that she is afraid of moving?" She then continued, stopping on page 7 to ask, "Do you think Simon wants to move? What do you think might happen next?" She continued reading to page 27 and asked, "How do you think the story will end?"

Once the story was finished, students checked the accuracy of their predictions. To bring the DLTA to a close, Shauna asked students to discuss who they think didn't want to move—Maggie or Simon—and to give reasons for their answers. She then invited them to state some suggestions for ways that Simon could confront his fear of moving. She concluded the DLTA by stating,

> Rather than telling readers what the character is like, authors most often show what characters are like through their actions and words. We need to use this information to form our ideas about the characters and why they are doing what they are doing. We have to "read between the lines."

Extensions/Tips/Connections

- The DLTA can be used to help students who have difficulty reading in content areas. Students can preread questions at the end of a given text and listen to the teacher read various sections of the text. At the end of each section, students can peruse their questions to see which,

if any, have been answered.
- Gillet and Temple (1994) suggest that the DLTA be used to assess students' orientation to stories. After a part of the story has been read, they suggest that students be invited to make predictions and that the teacher use questions such as the following to determine who is developing story sense:
  - Do they make predictions?
  - If so, are the predictions
    - wild and random?
    - based on what might actually happen in real life?
    - based on the logic of the story?
- Can they give reasons for their predictions?

Look for the Signals

Grade Levels: 1–5

Description

Typographical signals are used to help readers better understand an author's intended message. Commas, for example, signal when to pause to create the intended meaning (see examples that follow). With this procedure, the teacher selects specific sentences within a text and shows students how punctuation and other typographic signals, such as punctuation marks, large and bold print, underlining, and italics, or any combination of these signals, affect meaning.

Teaching Suggestions

1. Select specific sentences from a book children have read or will be reading that correspond to the specific signals to which you want students to attend. Figure 2–3 lists several signals and what they are intended to convey. Each can provide a focused, clear minilesson for students.

2. Using an overhead projector or chart paper, enlarge the passage that contains the sentences that provide the typographic signals you wish to call attention to. You may also wish to use big books that show the specific examples.

3. Tell students that you will read the sentence(s) two times and that you want them to listen to see which reading gives them the best idea about the character or event. In a monotone, read the sentence(s) to the students. Reread the sentence, using all typographic signals. Ask students to point out the differences: Which reading interested them more? Did emphasizing different words and pausing at different times give them a better understanding of what the author was trying to convey? Finally, point out the different typographic signals that you used and how these helped you to better convey the author's intended meaning.

Signal	What It Conveys	Example
Comma	Need for pause; placement affects meaning	Bill, my son is as big as you. Bill, my son, is as big as you.
Period	Need a longer pause	They sky looked mysterious.
Question mark	Need to raise intonation at the end of the sentence	Will you really?
Exclamation mark	Need to read with a certain emotion	It's a wonderful surprise!
Underlined, enlarged, and/or bold print	Need for special stress	This is what I believe. This is what I believe.
Combination	Used to show meaningful units	The teacher commented, "I am SO thrilled with this surprise!"

Figure 2–3. *Typographic Signals and What They Convey*

4. Provide students with meaningful practice and tell them to be "on the lookout" when reading to themselves.

5. When the silent reading period ends, have students read aloud one or more sentences in which they used a typographical signal and state what they believe the signal indicated they needed to do.

Suggested Titles

Title	Author (Last, First)	Publisher/Year ISBN	Suggested Grade Levels
"Dear Friend": Thomas Garrett and William Still	Bentley, Judith	Cobblehill/1997 052565156X	4–5
The Race of the Century	Downard, Barry	Simon & Schuster/2008 9781416925095	K–3
Beetle Bop	Fleming, Denise	Harcourt/2007 9780152059361	K–2

Title	Author (Last, First)	Publisher/Year ISBN	Suggested Grade Levels
Roller Coaster	Frazee, Marla	Harcourt/2003 0152045546	K–2
Arnie the Doughnut	Keller, Laurie	Holt/2003 0805062831	1–4
Bubble Bath Pirates	Krosoczka, Jarrett J.	Viking/2003 0670035998	K–1
The Ghost of Sifty-Sifty Sam	Medearis, Angela S.	Scholastic/1997 0590482904	2–4
Little Blue Truck	Schertle, Alice	Harcourt/2008 9780152056612	K–2
Smash! Crash!	Scieszka, Jon	Simon & Schuster/2008 9781416941330	K–2
Help Me Mr. Mutt!	Stevens, Janet	Harcourt/2008 9780152046286	1–4

Teacher Voices

Pat used *Oops!* (McNaughton 1997) to help her second graders learn how authors use typographical signals to convey meaning. First she read the story aloud to her class, reading softly when the words appeared small and loudly when they increased in size. After she had read the entire book, she went back to the pages to show how the words were written with small or large type. She explained that the size of the words helped her determine just how she should use her voice. She also noted that using her voice in these different ways helped her to better understand what the author was trying to communicate. She then reread the book and invited the children to read the words printed in large type when she pointed to them. She concluded the lesson by saying, "Today, when you are reading your books, pay attention to the way the words are written. If you see them in large type, this is the author's way of telling you to read the word with a lot of power so that you will get the right idea about the character who is speaking or the event that is happening."

Extensions/Tips/Connections

Students can find their own examples of typographic signals, write on their bookmarks the pages on which they occur, and share these examples during class discussion. Add some of their examples to the chart in Figure 2–3, or create a new one and display it in the classroom. This student-generated chart will be a meaningful reference when needed.

Say It Like the Character

Grade Levels: 1–8

Description

Often students can misinterpret or miss the author's intended meaning because they read silently the same way they read orally—in monotone. They may be approaching reading with a "crack the code" rather than "understand the message" mindset. They fail to understand that as the plot develops, so do the characters. What these students need to learn is that sometimes the author provides explicit help by using dialogue and words that describe feelings (e.g., "Jeff begged his father . . ."). Other times, however, the reader has to make inferences about how the character is speaking and feeling. *Say It Like the Character* helps students learn to make these inferences. This technique provides students with practice in learning how to infer both intonation and feelings so that they can better understand the intended meaning and, when appropriate, communicate this interpretation to others when reading aloud. Students are expected to read passages the way they think a character might actually speak to convey a specific, meaningful message.

Teaching Suggestions

1. Invite students to silently read a given text.
2. Identify a passage and ask students to silently reread it just the way they think the character might make it sound.
3. Ask a student to read the passage aloud, paying attention to how the character might actually say it—how the character might really feel about it.
4. Ask questions such as these: "What emotion were you trying to convey when you were reading?" "What made you think that you should have read it the way you did?" Both of these questions invite students to tell how they connect their own experiences with the character's. When reading the part of the monster in *The Hungry*

Monster (Root 1997), for example, students may state that they raise their voices when they get angry. Because the monster was angry, they knew how the monster was feeling and decided that the monster would show his anger by speaking loudly, just as they would. Students may also point out that surface-level features, such as enlarged or italic print, also provided a visual reminder of how to use their voices.

Suggested Titles

Title	Author (Last, First)	Publisher/Year ISBN	Suggested Grade Levels
The Tallest Tree	Belton, Sandra	Greenwillow/2008 9780060527501	3–7
Waiting for Normal	Connor, Leslie	Katherine Tegen/2008 9780060890896	5–8
The Cow That Laid an Egg	Cutbill, Andy	HarperCollins/2006 9780061372957	K–3
Ever-Clever Elisa	Hurwitz, Johanna	HarperCollins/2002 006441096X	1–2
My Favorite Thing (According to Alberta)	Jenkins, Emily	Atheneum/2004 0689849753	K–3
Shake Rag: From the Life of Elvis Presley	Littlesugar, Amy	Philomel/1998 039923005X	4–7
How I Became a Pirate	Long, Melinda	Harcourt/2003 0152018484	K–3
Sam Tells Stories	Robberecht, Thierry	Clarion/2007 9780618732807	K–2
Lila Bloom	Stadler, Alexander	Frances Foster/2003 0374344744	K–3
Winning Season: Curveball	Wallace, Rich	Puffin/2007 9780142410929	3–6

Teacher Voices

Carl's second-grade students enjoy reading books by Robert Munsch. Therefore, he decided to use Munsch's *Alligator Baby* (1997) to help students learn to read just like the character might talk to better help them comprehend and enjoy the story. He provided students with the necessary time to read the book silently. Next, he turned to specific pages and asked volunteers to read a given part the way that they thought the character would actually say the part if actually present in the classroom. Finally, he asked readers to state reasons for reading the way they did. Here are a couple of their responses:

> I knew that Kristen was feeling upset because her parents didn't believe her because that's how I feel when I am telling the truth and my parents won't believe me.

> I'll bet it hurt when the alligator bit Kristen's mother on the nose. I also saw the word *yelled*. These are the reasons I yelled the word *Aaaaahh-haaa!*

Carl closed the lesson by stating, "Today, when you are reading, pay attention to what is happening in the story, the pictures, the way the words are written, and the punctuation marks. All of these are ways that the author is trying to help you understand the characters and how they are feeling. It also helps to use what you know about the situation to help you best understand."

Extensions/Tips/Connections

- If students need additional practice on using expression when reading, you can have them think of a time when they were feeling a certain way—happy, sad, excited, afraid. Have them say the sentence with one of these emotions in mind. Using a tape recorder can help students actually hear the different ways they used their voices to express themselves.

• Mary Person (1990) describes another way to complete this procedure. She prints onto cards words that convey specific emotions
(e.g., fear, love, excitement, joy, anger) and prints sentences on sentence strips. Students are expected to choose one emotion card and
one sentence strip and read the sentence using the emotion stated on
the emotion card. We suggest using sentences from familiar books so
that students see the connection with this activity and how it relates
to reading.

Rapid Retrieval of Information (RRI)

Grade Levels: 3–8

Description

Skimming to locate specific information requires students to distinguish relevant information from irrelevant information. It is an important strategy to use for previewing and reviewing material and for quickly locating information to verify or support a point of view. It is also one way that we read in our everyday lives. For example, we skim the newspaper, looking for articles of most interest, and skim the phone book to locate a specific phone number. *Rapid Retrieval of Information* (RRI) (Green 1998) helps students learn this most important strategy. It calls on students to orally reread information gleaned from the text that provides an answer to a question or helps to prove a point. First, students read the material silently and then reread portions of the text that correspond to one or more tasks provided by the teacher.

Teaching Suggestions

1. Provide students with a text to read, and provide in-class time for them to read it silently.

2. Once silent reading has occurred, present a specific task individually. Sample tasks include asking children to read aloud a sentence that explains how a character was treated, to identify information that proves a given point, and to find a phrase that defines a specific word.

3. Ask students to listen to the task and reread appropriate parts of the text in search of information that addresses the task at hand.

4. Once students have located the information, they signal, and one is called upon to read aloud to the class.

Suggested Titles

Title	Author (Last, First)	Publisher/Year ISBN	Suggested Grade Levels
She Touched the World: Laura Bridgman, Deaf-Blind Pioneer	Alexander, Sally H.	Clarion/2008 9780618852994	5–8
Ballpark: The Story of America's Baseball Fields	Curlee, Lynn	Aladdin/2008 9781416953609	4–7
Who Was Sacagawea?	Fradin, Judith B.	Grosset & Dunlap/2002 0448424851	3–5
Water Buffalo Days	Huynh, Quang N.	HarperCollins/1999 0064462110	3–4
Albert Einstein: A Biography	Meltzer, Milton	Holiday House/2008 9780823419661	5–7
A New Beginning, Celebrating the Spring Equinox	Pfeffer, Wendy	Dutton/2008 9780525478744	2–3
African Americans Who Were First	Potter, Joan	Cobblehill/1997 0525652469	3–5
Sharks! Strange and Wonderful	Pringle, Laurence	Boyds Mills/2008 9781590785713	3–5
An Island Grows	Schaefer, Lola M.	Greenwillow/2006 9780066239309	K–2
Elizabeth Leads the Way	Stone, Tanya L.	Holt/2008 9780805079036	2–4

Teacher Voices

As part of a larger unit on slavery, Marilyn's students were reading *Slavery Time: When I Was Chillun* (Hurmence 1997). To help her students learn to skim more efficiently for specific information, she decided to use RRI along with this book. She provided her class with some time to read the first chapter silently, providing assistance when needed. She then asked students to reread the text for specific information. She used prompts such as these:

- Find the sentence that describes James Bolton's house.
- Compare the types of houses in which James and his master lived. Be ready to read sentences that support your answer.
- Did James think it was better to be free or to be a slave? Locate sentences that support your answer.

She concluded the lessons by stating, "Many times when we read, we are looking for specific information. When this is the purpose for reading, you will not read every word. Instead, you will look for the parts that provide you with the information you need."

Extensions/Tips/Connections

- When first attempting this activity, use text that is fairly easy for students to read so that they can focus on learning the procedures associated with the activity. If you are using text of more than one page, telling students where to focus will ensure their success from the start.
- To show students how skimming relates to other reading strategies, you may want to try TAG: Textbook Activity Guide (Johns and Lenski 1997). After determining the material to be read by students, these authors suggest that you design the TAG so that students learn to interact with the text in several ways. Here's an example:

  Predict: Survey the headings on pages 10–13. Write what you think you will learn by reading this chapter.

  Read and Discuss: Read the introduction on page 10 and tell the person next to you what you think you already know about the information to be presented in the chapter.

  Skim: Skim pages 11 and 12.

  Read and Retell: Read pages 13 and 14 silently. Retell in writing everything you have learned up to this point.

Read to Discover

Grade Levels: 1–3

Description

You can use *Read to Discover*, a variation of Rapid Retrieval of Information (see page 36), in the primary grades to help students learn to locate information that relates to a given prompt. For example, you can ask students to reread to discover an exciting part, a given statement that answers a specific question, or their favorite part. Students can also identify passages that they find especially meaningful and provide reasons for their choices. You can use this strategy to help students identify pertinent information in stories as well as in nonfiction text. As with Rapid Retrieval of Information, this strategy helps students learn how to skim text, which is one way that we read in everyday life.

Teaching Suggestions

1. Write several prompts on individual cards. Some of these prompts might be open-ended and work with any reading selection. Others might focus on a specific book you want children to read. For example, when reading *Willy's Silly Grandma* (DeFelice 1997), "Read to find the part you liked best" is an open-ended prompt. "Find the sentence that tells where Willy's grandfather first told him that he'd better not call his grandmother silly" is a prompt related to this book only.
2. Place all of these cards in a "prompt" container.
3. Explain the teaching procedure to the students. You might say, "Today we're going to practice looking for specific information from the story we will be reading. After you have read this story silently, I am going to pull one card from this prompt container, read it, and give you time to find the information that answers the prompt."
4. Provide students with the text they are to read and allow them some time to read it silently.

5. Once silent reading has occurred, read students a prompt—or choose a student to read the prompt—and have the rest of the children in the group or class locate the appropriate information.
6. Students then signal when they have located the information, and one is chosen to read aloud.

Suggested Titles

Title	Author (Last, First)	Publisher/Year ISBN	Suggested Grade Levels
Babies in the Bayou	Arnosky, Jim	G. P. Putnam's Sons/2007 9780399226533	K–1
The Brook Book: Exploring the Smallest Streams	Arnosky, Jim	Dutton/2008 9780525477167	2–4
Walking Through the Jungle	Blackstone, Stella	Barefoot Books/2006 1905236999	1–2
Stick	Breen, Steve	Dial/2007 9780803731240	K–2
Willy's Silly Grandma	DeFelice, Cynthia C.	Orchard/1997 0531300129	2–3
Oodles of Animals	Ehlert, Lois	Harcourt/2008 9780152062743	K–2
The Planets	Gibbons, Gail	Holiday House/2008 9780823421566	1–3
Close to You	Kajikawa, Kimiko	Holt/2008 9780805081237	K–1
Chidi Only Likes Blue	Onyefulu, Ifeoma	Frances Lincoln/2006 1845075137	1–2
President's Day	Rockwell, Anne	HarperCollins/2008 9780060501952	K–2

Teacher Voices

After having all of her students read *The Chocolate Touch* (Catling 1952), Carol provided a review activity for her students by constructing a large chocolate kiss. She printed specific prompts on slips of paper and placed these in the kiss so that she could select them with ease—similar to pulling the paper to unwrap a real chocolate kiss. Students were provided time to respond to the prompt. Sample prompts included the following:

- Find the part where you were first convinced that John loved candy above all else.
- Find one part where you felt sorry for John.

She concluded by commenting, "Sharing favorite parts of books is something readers do. Knowing how to find parts that are meaningful to you helps you to communicate with others. This is part of what it means to be a reader!"

Extensions/Tips/Connections

- Once students are familiar with this activity, teach them how to write prompts and, when appropriate, the page numbers on which their prompts are answered. Place their prompts in the container and use them when doing this activity.
- Many times, responses to questions do not reside with the text alone. You may want to teach students about question-answer relationships (QARs) (Raphael 1982) to help them understand how different questions need to be answered. "Right there" are questions whose answers are explicitly stated in the text. "Think and Search" are questions that have ideas stated in the text but in different places. The reader has to locate and put these ideas together to answer the question. "Author and You" and "On My Own" are questions that have answers that are not stated explicitly in the text. The reader has to use prior knowledge and experience to answer the question. Raphael (1982, 1986) offers ideas for teaching these relationships to children.

CHAPTER 3

Sharing and Performing

No doubt about it! Although we primarily read silently in our everyday lives, we do have occasion to read aloud; for example, we might recite a poem, share a funny cartoon from the daily comics, or read a letter from grandma to other family members. And we frequently hear examples of reading aloud—for instance, the news reporters broadcasting their stories over the radio or on the evening news. Certainly the actors we watch on stage at our local theatre or on a television sitcom spent hours reading and memorizing their lines to achieve the right delivery and emotion. Clearly, when oral reading is used for authentic purposes, students have reason to read with good expression and sense of meaning, the keys to good oral reading.

The purpose of this chapter is to show how we can use oral reading authentically—for sharing and performing. Figure 3–1 provides an overview of the oral reading strategies presented in this chapter and the skills that each strategy helps children develop. *Preparation* and *audience* are two key words to keep in mind when using these oral reading strategies. Because the intent of these activities is to share and communicate information, readers need time to prepare their presentations. And when readers are expected to perform, they also need an interested audience.

Reading Skills/Strategies	Effective Oral Reading Strategies						
	Revised Radio Reading	Shared Book Experience	Choral Reading	Mentor Reading	Readers Theatre	Read Around	Poetry Club
Positive attitude/Interest in reading	•	•	•	•	•	•	•
Reading comprehension	•	•	•	•	•	•	•
Listening comprehension	•	•			•		•
Vocabulary	•	•	•	•	•	•	•
Use of language cueing systems	•	•	•	•	•	•	•
Predicting		•		•	•		
Forming images	•		•	•	•		•
Using prior knowledge	•	•	•	•	•		•
Monitoring	•			•	•		
Inferring	•	•	•	•	•		•
Expression (fluency)	•		•	•	•	•	•
Phrasing (fluency)	•	•	•	•	•	•	•
Skimming							

Figure 3–1. *Effective Oral Reading Strategies and Skills for Developing Comprehension*

Revised Radio Reading

Grade Levels: 1–5

Description

Revised Radio Reading (Greene 1979; Searfoss 1975) is a good alternative to round robin reading. Students perform preselected portions of a text that they have had the opportunity to rehearse. While one reader reads—taking on the role of radio announcer—others take on the role of listeners in much the same way as people might listen to a story told over the radio. At the end of the reading, the reader leads the group in a brief discussion of the passage. All in all, Radio Reading offers a much more viable, satisfying, and instructionally appropriate approach to oral reading.

Teaching Suggestions (based on Searfoss 1975)

1. In our adaptation of Radio Reading, the day before the experience is to occur, the teacher looks over a text selection and provides students with a brief overview of it. The teacher then divides the text into enough sections so that each member of the group has a section.

2. In preparation for the Radio Reading experience, students rehearse their assigned sections. This can be accomplished in school, at home, or both. The readers also prepare for a brief discussion for their section of the story by developing open-ended questions or provocative statements about the section that will induce the audience to talk.

3. On the day for the assigned Radio Reading, review the Radio Reading procedures with students. Remind audience members that they should have their books closed so that they can listen while the student-reader presents a passage. Introduce the selection or ask another student to make the introduction. Then the student assigned the first section of the passage reads as expressively and meaningfully as possible while the others listen. The first student's reading ends with a brief discussion of that section of the passage. You may also choose to postpone the discussion until the entire text has been read.

4. After the first reader, the other readers in the group read their sections in order while the other students listen.

5. If you choose to do Radio Reading on the following day, students should discuss and be assigned or self-select their sections for the following period.

Suggested Titles

You can easily use Radio Reading with literature-based basal readers or with children's trade books. However, we have found that Radio Reading works particularly well with beginning chapter books in which each chapter tells a small story.

Title	Author (Last, First)	Publisher/Year ISBN	Suggested Grade Levels
A Beginning, a Muddle, and an End: The Right Way to Write Writing	Avi	Harcourt/2008 9780152055554	2–5
Ramona Quimby, Age 8	Cleary, Beverly	HarperCollins/1981 0380709562	2–5
My Chocolate Year	Herman, Charlotte	Simon & Schuster/2008 9781416933410	3–7
Days with Frog and Toad	Lobel, Arnold	HarperCollins/1984 0064440583	1–2
One Voice, Please: Favorite Read-Aloud Stories	McBratney, Sam	Candlewick/2005 9780763634797	2–5
Dragon's Fat Cat	Pilkey, Dav	Scholastic/1995 0531070689	1–3
Pizza, Pigs, and Poetry: How to Write a Poem	Prelutsky, Jack	Greenwillow/2008 9780061434495	3–8
The Redheaded Princess	Rinaldi, Ann	HarperCollins/2008 9780060733759	5–8

Title	Author (Last, First)	Publisher/Year ISBN	Suggested Grade Levels
Henry and Mudge Take the Big Test	Rylant, Cynthia	Simon & Schuster/1996 9780689808869	1–3
Encyclopedia Brown Saves the Day	Sobol, Donald J.	Puffin/1970 9780142409213	2–4

Teacher Voices

Janet has taught in the primary grades for more than fifteen years. Although she had sometimes used round robin reading, she had never felt comfortable with it. She learned about Radio Reading at an inservice and decided to give it a try. In her words,

> Things always seemed to go wrong when I used round robin reading. I spent a lot more time monitoring the children and their behavior than I did on the reading itself. Radio Reading is better. Now students actually have an opportunity to practice what they are going to read beforehand. And, while one student reads, the others listen. It permits me to observe my readers in a way that makes more sense than what I had been doing. I have noticed that many of my most quiet and fearful students are no longer fearful about reading aloud. I'm convinced that giving them time to practice before reading to others is what has helped them to get over their fears.

Extensions/Tips/Connections

Radio Reading can easily lead into performing for other audiences. Indeed, Janet's students used an old refrigerator box to make a large old-fashioned radio. Whenever they perform Radio Reading for other students, they drag out the "radio" and place it in front of the group. The karaoke machine that Janet purchased is also used. The microphone is attached to a pole stand. About once each month, different groups of students perform Radio Reading for others in the class. Individual readers stand and read into the microphone in much the same way old-time radio performers did.

Shared Book Experience

Grade Levels: K–2 (Primarily; however, it can also be used with more sophisticated texts in the upper grades. Students can be invited to interact with the teacher as she reads a given text.)

Description

During *Shared Book Experience* (SBE) the teacher reads a text to children and invites them to read along when they can. Both teacher and students read orally using a book large enough for all to see. The teacher can use the experience to focus on any number of print concepts, such as left-to-right progression and reading top to bottom. Repeated readings and discussions of the books or chart stories will help students learn to read with expression and allow for deeper levels of comprehension. In fact, research has shown that SBE is an excellent way to develop students' ability to analyze words and their literal and inferential comprehension (Reutzel, Hollingsworth, and Eldredge 1994).

Teaching Suggestions (based on Holdaway 1979)

1. Introduce the book by talking about the title, author's name, and so forth. Invite students to tell what they think this book might be about.
2. Read the story aloud to the students while they listen. Point to words as they are read in order to demonstrate that the written words convey the book's message and that readers need to attend to the text.
3. Reread the story several times over several days. Invite students to read along if they wish. As students become more proficient with the text, allow individual students to read. Keep the text on display throughout the school day so that students can read it on their own.
4. Encourage students to talk about the story—likes, what they noticed, funny parts, scary parts.

5. You may wish to move on to smaller versions of the same story. Students can read the text on their own and even take it home to share with others.

6. Even after you have read the text over several days, return to it occasionally for rereading. This conveys to students that good books are meant to be read and enjoyed more than once!

Suggested Titles

Title	Author (Last, First)	Publisher/Year ISBN	Suggested Grade Levels
Rain Play	Cotten, Cynthia	Holt/2008 9780805067958	K–2
On the Farm	Elliott, David	Candlewick/2008 9780763633226	K–2
Traces	Fox, Paula	Front Street/2008 9781932425437	1–3
Only One Neighborhood	Garrison, Barbara	Dutton/2007 9780525474685	K–2
Red Truck	Hamilton, Kersten	Viking/2008 9780670062751	K–1
A Closer Look	McCarthy, Mary	Greenwillow/2007 9780061240737	K–3
One Duck Stuck: A Mucky Duck Counting Book	Root, Phyllis	Candlewick/2008 9780763638177 (Big Book)	K–2
One Tractor: A Counting Book	Siy, Alexandra	Holiday House/2008 9780823419234	K–1
Everywhere the Cow Says, "Moo!"	Weinstein, Ellen S.	Boyds Mills/2008 9781590784587	K–3
Tracks in the Snow	Wong, Herbert Y.	Holt/2003 080506771X	K–2

Teacher Voices

Josh called his first graders to the meeting area for a group read of Miranda's *To Market, to Market* (1997). He followed all of the previously mentioned strategies but enlisted a student to help him when reading the story a second time. "Paul, could you help me point to the words?" Paul eagerly volunteered and pointed with ease as the other students read along. Josh commented, "It is so gratifying to use this type of oral reading. Every member of the class can participate at some level. All students experience some level of success. I can't imagine teaching first grade without this fun way of engaging all students."

Extensions/Tips/Connections

When children have independent reading time, invite them to read books introduced during the SBE. They may choose to read alone, with a partner, or with a group of interested classmates. If the book is on tape or CD, you might want to make these available for students who want to use them.

Choral Reading

Grade Levels: 1–5

Description

As in the SBE, *Choral Reading* involves groups of students orally reading one text together. And as in choral singing, the group works
together to make a meaningful and enjoyable performance. Because the
text is read or performed as a group, Choral Reading is a superb way to
build teamwork during reading. Moreover, because all students read
during Choral Reading, all students grow as readers. And, for those students who may be a bit reticent to perform on their own, or may have
some difficulty in reading, the support from the entire group of readers
allows all readers to be successful. The choral voice is usually very
pleasing to the ear and lends itself to performance for groups.

Teaching Suggestions

1. Select a text to be read as a group in unison. Poems, predictable
   books, and ritual text, such as the Pledge of Allegiance, are excellent
   choices.
2. Make the text visually accessible to every member of the group.
   This can be done by putting the text on a transparency and pro-
   jecting it via an overhead projector, writing it on chart paper, or
   providing each student in the group with a conventionally sized
   version of the text.
3. Model Choral Reading by first reading the text aloud to students. Be
   sure to discuss with the group how you use your voice to express
   meaning. (See *Look for the Signals* in Chapter 2.)
4. Read the text chorally several times over several days. When visi-
   tors come into the class, use the opportunity to perform the reading for them.

Suggested Titles

Title	Author (Last, First)	Publisher/Year ISBN	Suggested Grade Levels
Bringing the Rain to Kapiti Plain	Aardema, Verna	Dial/1981 0803708092	2–3
Up, Down, and Around	Ayres, Katherine	Candlewick/2007 9780763640187 (Big Book)	K–2
Who Ate All the Cookie Dough?	Beaumont, Karen	Holt/2008 9780805082678	K–2
Mother Goose, Numbers on the Loose	Dillon, Leo	Harcourt/2007 9780152056766	K–1
Here Is the Wetland	Dunphy, Margaret	Hyperion/1996 0786821361	2–3
Scoot!	Falwell, Cathryn	Greenwillow/2008 9780061288821	K–3
Joyful Noise	Fleischman, Paul	Harper & Row/1988 0060218525	4–5
Monkey and Me	Gravett, Emily	Simon & Schuster/2007 9781416954576	K–1
Chicken Soup with Rice	Sendak, Maurice	HarperTrophy/1991 9780064432535	1–2
If I Were in Charge of the World and Other Worries	Viorst, Judith	Simon & Schuster/1984 0689707703	1–3

Teacher Voices

Sandra uses Choral Reading with her third graders nearly every day. Here's what she has to say about it:

> Some of my colleagues ask me why I continue to use Choral Reading with third graders. They say, "Aren't they a little old for that?" I don't think

there's any age when Choral Reading is inappropriate. Choral Reading is a way for all of us to do something together. I tell my class that we are a team and that this is one way that we can act as a team. Those children who are having trouble in reading can still feel success without having to be embarrassed by reading out loud on their own. We'll read a short poem or other text once, twice, even three times. And, by the time we are at the third reading, nearly all of my students can read the passage easily and fluently, even those who find reading difficult.

Sandra usually chooses poems for Choral Reading. "I have several poetry anthologies on my desk, and I can usually find something to go along with the season, holiday, or mood of the class." She also uses poems written by her students, selections from books, and song lyrics. Many times she invites students to choose the texts they want to read chorally.

Extensions/Tips/Connections

Jeannette Miccinati (1985) offers numerous ways to do Choral Reading. *Refrain*, in which children join together in the reading of a refrain, is the easiest to learn. In *Line-a-Child*, each child is given a line to read and reads at the appropriate time. With *Antiphonal* reading, children are divided into two groups, and each group reads assigned parts alternately. *Unison*, in which the entire class reads the text together, is perhaps the most difficult in that all readers have to stay together and place the same emphasis at given points throughout the reading.

Mentor Reading

Grade Levels: 1–5

Description

Mentor Reading is a way for children to read with a mentor in such a way that the mentor provides support, or scaffolding, for the reader. That mentor can be a teacher, parent at home, parent volunteer in the classroom, older student tutor, or even a classmate. Through Mentor Reading, students are invited to read challenging texts. The key characteristic of Mentor Reading is that it takes place between two readers sitting side by side. Although Mentor Reading involves an oral performance of sorts, it takes place in a private setting so that the partner is the only audience.

Teaching Suggestions

1. People who serve as reading mentors need training in how to work with and respond to their partners. Mentors are instructed in the shared reading format, encouraged to be kind and patient with the students, and shown how to provide support to the student reader when it is necessary—offering only enough support to allow the student to be successful.
2. Assign student readers a partner mentor (e.g., parent volunteer, older student, classmate). Set times for the Mentor Reading. It usually works best in short periods (i.e., from ten to thirty minutes).
3. Students should choose their own texts; however, the mentor should have some input into the selection.
4. During the Mentor Reading period, students and mentors find a comfortable and private spot in which to read together.
5. Call time a few minutes before the end of the period so that the partners have a few minutes to talk about the reading before moving on to another activity.

Suggested Titles

Just about any title that the student chooses can be used for Mentor Reading. Page 62 lists reference books that offer a wealth of titles for interesting reading.

Teacher Voices

Nancy asks her parent volunteer to do Mentor Reading with her fourth-grade students. She comments, "It's easy to learn and implement. Students and parents enjoy it, and my parent volunteers can come into class knowing exactly what to do with their assigned students. Best of all, I have seen my students make a tremendous amount of progress as a result of the extra reading that Mentor Reading provides."

Extensions/Tips/Connections

- *Echo Reading* is one variation of Mentor Reading. In Echo Reading, a mentor reads a phrase or sentence, and the student rereads, or echoes, the same text.
- First-grade teacher Jeanne has connected her class with Joyce's fourth graders for the past several years. Twice a week, the two classes meet in the school cafeteria. Each of Jeanne's students is paired with a mentor from Joyce's class. Students bring blankets, pillows, stuffed animals, and, of course, books in order to make the cafeteria a comfortable place for reading. During the thirty-minute Mentor Reading period, the first graders and their mentors read one of the books. Sometimes the younger student reads to the mentor. Other times, the mentor reads to the first grader.

Readers Theatre

Grade Levels: 1–5

Description

Readers Theatre is a way for groups of students to use their reading voices to perform a story or script for an audience. Unlike classroom plays, Readers Theatre does not require extensive preparatory work on the part of the teacher. Using plays in the classroom can be a logistical nightmare for one person because of the many details associated with putting on a play. In Readers Theatre, students do not memorize lines, and they do not use sets, props, or costumes. They are not required to move around on a stage. Instead, the cast simply stands in front of the audience and reads aloud from a script. Because no overt sets, props, or costumes are used, the only way for the cast to convey the meaning of the script is through their reading voices. Thus, they must read with meaning and expression. Readers Theatre promotes students' fluent, expressive, and meaningful reading.

Teaching Suggestions

1. Select the material you want students to read or have them choose their own material. The key to successful Readers Theatre experiences is to find appropriate texts or scripts—texts that lend themselves to being read aloud. Scripts are relatively easy to find, for example, in basal readers and in magazines. There are also book collections of scripts (see suggested titles that follow). Moreover, many children's books are written in ways that make them perfect for a Readers Theatre presentation. Angela Johnson's *Tell Me a Story, Mama* (1989), for example, lends itself to having two students present it to the rest of the class. One can take on the role of mother, and the other, the role of daughter. Paul Fleischman's *Bull Run* (1995) tells the story of the first battle of the Civil War from the points of view of various participants and observers. It could be

presented easily by having different students perform the roles of the different characters.

2. Give an overview of the text(s) and divide students into groups, making sure that there are enough members for each character in the script.

3. Provide students with time to read their scripts silently. Students will need to practice the scripts both individually and as a group to ensure that they are ready to present their "play" before an audience. This repeated practice provides students with an opportunity to develop many skills associated with good reading—fluency, reading with expression, and greater sensitivity to the author's intended meaning, to name a few.

4. Have the group perform for the class when they feel that they are ready. These performances can be scheduled throughout the week, or you may want to have them presented at a designated time on a given day.

5. After the group performs, you may want to have the audience respond to the play or parts of the play. Here are a couple of response ideas:
   • Provide students with blank pieces of paper and have them draw what they think a given character or scene from the story looks like, based on the description they heard in the story.
   • Ask students to write three words that they think best describe a character.

Suggested Titles

Collections of Scripts for Use in Readers Theatre

Title	Author (Last, First)	Publisher/Year ISBN
Fifty Fabulous Fables: Beginning Readers Theatre	Barchers, Suzanne	Libraries Unlimited/1997 9781563085536
Frantic Frogs and Other Frankly Fractured Folktales for Readers Theatre	Fredericks, Anthony D.	Libraries Unlimited/1993 9781563081743

Title	Author (Last, First)	Publisher/Year ISBN
Cinderella Outgrows the Glass Slipper and Other Zany Fractured Fairy Tale Plays: 5 Funny Plays with Related Writing Activities and Graphic Organizers That Motivate Kids to Explore Plot, Characters, and Settings	Wolf, Joan M.	Scholastic/2002 9780439271684
Readers Theater for Building Fluency: Strategies and Scripts for Making the Most of This Highly Effective, Motivating, and Research-Based Approach to Oral Reading	Worthy, Jo	Scholastic/2005 9780439522236

Children's Books

Title	Author (Last, First)	Publisher/Year ISBN	Suggested Grade Levels
This Little Piggy's Book of Manners	Allen, Kathryn M.	Holt/2003 0805067698	2–3
The Pain and the Great One	Blume, Judy	Random House/1985 9780440409670	1–3
Hurry! Hurry!	Bunting, Eve	Harcourt/2007 9780152054106	K
Where Are You Going? To See My Friend!	Carle, Eric	Orchard/2001 0439416590	1–2
Bull Run	Fleischman, Paul	HarperCollins/1995 0064405885	4–5
Leaving the Nest	Gerstein, Mordicai	Frances Foster/2007 9780374343699	2–3
Go Track a Yak!	Johnston, Tony	Simon & Schuster/2003 0689837895	3–5

Title	Author (Last, First)	Publisher/Year ISBN	Suggested Grade Levels
Jack and Jill	Kirk, Daniel	G. P. Putnam's Sons/2003 0399235531	2–3
How Hungry Are You?	Napoli, Donna	Atheneum/2001 068983389X	1–3
Wee Little Chick	Thompson, Lauren	Simon & Schuster/2008 9781416934684	K–1

Teacher Voices

Laura uses Readers Theatre as a way to provide all readers with a meaningful way to develop fluency. After one especially good experience, she and her students took the performance "on the road." They performed for nearly every classroom in the school, the Parent Teacher Association, the school board, and the local senior center. Laura commented,

> Every performance was a rousing success. These kids really learned how to perform, and each performance got better. Their reading of this script and others improved markedly over the two weeks we did this activity. Best of all, though, was the change in the children's attitudes toward reading. Many of the students who were performing sometimes forget that the purpose of reading is to understand. This activity sure helps them to see the importance of reading for meaning. And who knows? Maybe Readers Theatre is the start for some budding actors!

Extensions/Tips/Connections

• If Readers Theatre is new to your students, prepare a script with colleagues and perform it for your students. When you have finished the performance, talk with your students about how you prepared for the experience—the amount of practicing you did, the way you experimented with your voice to get it just right—as well as what you had to keep in mind while performing (e.g., appropriate volume, expression).

- If you want students to learn how to write scripts or to learn how one style of writing can be changed into another style, you might give pairs of students a short story and show them how to turn it into a script. Students could then use their scripts for Readers Theatre. Lobel's book *Fables* (1980) is an excellent book to use for this purpose. This activity is especially well suited for students who have difficulty generating writing topics. The original text acts as a scaffold for students, who not only recast the story in script form, but also can add or delete portions from the text.
- *Learning with Readers Theatre* (Dixon, Davies, and Politano 1996) offers a wealth of ideas for teaching students about Readers Theatre.

Read Around

Grade Levels: K–5

Description

In the *Read Around*, students read their favorite sentences and/or paragraphs to others. Each student, in turn, identifies and rehearses a passage for the rest of the members in the group or class (Tompkins 1998). Sharing memorable and favorite passages inspires critical thinking and promotes fluent and meaningful reading.

Teaching Suggestions

1. Invite students to look back through something they have read previously to find at least one favorite sentence or paragraph that they would like to share with others. You can use nonfiction and fiction as well as a variety of reading materials—books, magazines, and comics, to name a few.
2. Once passages have been located, have students mark them by using a stick-on note or a slip of paper. Bookmarks could serve this purpose.
3. Provide students with time to rehearse the passage silently. Most will need to practice reading their passages at least two times.
4. Ask for one volunteer to read his passage to the group while the other students listen. The next student can then begin reading. Rather than calling on students, allow them to take their cues from one another and read when no one else is reading. Order is not important with this activity. Also keep in mind that you, the teacher, can read a passage.
5. Continue reading until every person who wishes to perform has had the opportunity.
6. Either before or at the end of the sharing, invite students to share why they chose their particular passages. This will help students to see that there are many ways to choose passages.

Suggested Titles

The following are references that provide excellent reading material for children:

Title	Author (Last, First)	Publisher/Year ISBN
Some of My Best Friends Are Books	Halsted, Judith W.	Great Potential/2002 9780910707510
Eyeopeners II: Children's Books to Answer Children's Questions About the World Around Them, K–12	Kobrin, Beverly	Scholastic/1995 9780590484022
Making the Match: The Right Book for the Right Reader at the Right Time, Grades 4–12	Lesesne, Teri S.	Stenhouse/2003 9781571103819
Getting the Most from Predictable Books	Opitz, Michael F.	Scholastic/1996 9780590270496
Books and Beyond: New Ways to Reach Readers	Opitz, Michael F., and Michael P. Ford	Heinemann/2006 9780325007434
Kaleidoscope: A Multicultural Booklist for Grades K–8	Yokota, Junko	National Council of Teachers of English/2001 978081412540

Teacher Voices

"Read Around was one of the first activities I used when I started to move away from round robin reading," Karen commented to Michael. She continued, "I find this to be a meaningful way to use oral reading because students get to choose the passages they want to read, and they get some time to practice reading to make sure that they can read it with ease. What I am finding is that students really listen to one another when passages are being shared."

Extensions/Tips/Connections

If students are new to this way of reading, you will want to ensure their success by providing them with some guidance. Have the children read and identify their passages from the same story. Have children close their books until it is their turn to share their favorite part.

Poetry Club

64
Good-bye
Round Robin

Grade Levels: 1–5

Description

Poetry is meant to be read aloud. Our appreciation for poetry arises not only from the poet's words, but also from the reader's voice. Poetry should play a central role in every elementary classroom. *Poetry Club* provides a forum for performing and celebrating poetry. It also creates authentic reasons for students to engage in practiced, repeated readings, a powerful way to help students develop sensitivity to their language. A more formal version of Read Around (see page 61), Poetry Club gives students opportunities to select, practice, and read a favorite poem to interested others.

Teaching Suggestions

1. Show students your love of poetry by ensuring that it is part of your classroom decor and library. Display poems on your bulletin boards. Have several collections of poetry in your classroom library. Display your favorite volume of poetry on your desk.
2. After reading aloud several poems to students, tell them that they will have the opportunity to look through the several poetry books you have displayed from which to choose their own poem to read to the class. Show students the various titles from which they may choose (see the following list of suggested titles).
3. Provide students with time to select and rehearse poems. If poem selection occurs on Monday, students could spend the remainder of the week practicing their poems; they can try out the poems in different voices, using different phrases, and at different rates. They need plenty of practice to get the poem "just right."
4. Invite students to sign up for reading their poems during Poetry Club, which can be held for a specified amount of time on Friday.

5. When Poetry Club time comes around, gather students in the meeting area of your classroom and have those that signed up share their poems. Students may want to include information about their poet and their reasons for choosing to share a given poem.

Suggested Titles

Title	Author (Last, First)	Publisher/Year ISBN	Suggested Grade Levels
Big Talk, Poems for Four Voices	Fleischman, Paul	Candlewick/2008 9780763638054	2–5
Bow Wow Meow Meow: It's Rhyming Cats and Dogs	Florian, Douglas	Harcourt/2003 0152163956	K–3
Home on the Range: Cowboy Poetry	Janeczko, Paul B.	Dial/1997 0803719108	3–8
Lift Every Voice and Sing	Johnson, James W.	Amistad/2007 9780060541477	K–5
Oops!	Katz, Alan	Margaret K. McElderry/2008 9781416902041	2–5
A Crossing of Zebras: Animal Packs in Poetry	Maddox, Marjorie	Wordsong/2008 9781590785102	K–4
Animals That Ought to Be	Michelson, Richard	Simon & Schuster/1996 0689806353	1–4
This Big Sky	Mora, Pat	Scholastic/2002 0439400708	1–4
My Dog May Be a Genius	Prelutsky, Jack	Greenwillow/2008 9780066238623	1–5
If: A Father's Advice to His Son	Smith, Charles R. Jr.	Atheneum/2007 9780689877994	3–8

Teacher Voices

Patsy and Brian have separate fifth-grade classes, but on Fridays, the classes come together for Poetry Club. Their classes take on the role of performers on alternate weeks. Club meetings last less than an hour, and every student who performs volunteers rather than being forced to share. Brian comments, "I think our students really enjoy the opportunity to perform for their classmates in the other class. It is very enlightening to watch them select the perfect poem and practice it all week. At first, students were reluctant to volunteer but not anymore! The main problem we now face is having enough time for all who've signed up to share." Patsy adds, "As the school year has progressed, students have learned to appreciate poetry. In fact, I have had several students write and perform their own poems. Sometimes students will choose to perform a poem together in unison or by taking parts. Charlie impressed all of us last week by adding a melody to his poem, turning it into a song!"

Extensions/Tips/Connections

Darlene's third graders also have a Poetry Club. Darlene's innovation includes creating an ambiance for the performances. She turns off the overhead lights and places a reading lamp on the "stage" to act as a spotlight. A reading stool completes the stage. The rest of the classroom is turned into a coffeehouse atmosphere by having students arrange their desks into groups to simulate tables. Refreshments are provided (juice and popcorn) while students, in turn, sit on the stool to read their poems. One day, one of the students' grandparents, who was a child of the 1950s, brought some of his favorite poems to share. He taught students how to snap their fingers as an alternative to clapping to show that they enjoyed the poem. Who knows? Poetry Clubs just may bring the beatnik era back to life!

CHAPTER 4

Helping Struggling Readers

*D*espite our best efforts, some students find learning to read difficult. For some students, misperceptions of reading and a limited repertoire of strategies to use when reading cause difficulty. These students fail to understand that the main purpose of reading is for understanding. Instead, they view reading as getting the words right, with little or no attention to what the words mean. They also fail to see that reading is language and that it should sound like language when reading. For others, comprehension and knowledge of word meanings can pose difficulties. For still other students, lack of fluency and insufficient word recognition may impede their reading development.

Oral reading is an effective way to help these children become stronger readers, as the twelve reasons in Chapter 1 verify. Two additional reasons that oral reading is especially effective for struggling readers are as follows:

1. Oral reading provides students with an avenue for monitoring their own reading. While reading aloud, students are able to hear themselves read and are more able to detect if their reading sounds like language and makes sense. If these readings are tape-recorded, students can analyze their own reading well after the reading has occurred. (See Chapter 5 for further explanations regarding assessment.) This ability to look upon their reading from a distance invites reflection.

2. Oral reading provides teachers with a way of assessing and supporting students' reading. Helping a child when she is reading silently is difficult because the teacher cannot determine when she needs help, unless she requests assistance. Oral reading enables the teacher to monitor her reading and provide help when needed. This help can take on a variety of forms: from asking her questions that help her use different language cues (see Chapter 1) to helping her learn to use a variety of reading strategies that focus on constructing meaning.

The oral reading strategies presented in this chapter can be especially helpful for children who struggle with reading. Figure 4–1 provides an overview of oral reading activities that are especially effective for helping children who find reading difficult. As with the other charts presented in Chapters 2 and 3, Figure 4–1 shows how these strategies help readers develop specific reading skills.

Effective Oral Reading Strategies

Reading Skills/Strategies	Read-Aloud	Paired Reading	Recorded Texts	Listen to Children Read	Fluency Development Lesson
Positive attitude/Interest in reading	•	•	•	•	•
Reading comprehension		•		•	•
Listening comprehension	•	•	•		•
Vocabulary	•	•	•	•	•
Use of language cueing systems		•		•	
Predicting	•	•	•	•	
Forming images	•	•	•		•
Using prior knowledge		•			
Monitoring		•		•	
Inferring		•		•	
Expression (fluency)	•	•	•	•	•
Phrasing (fluency)		•		•	
Skimming					

Figure 4–1. *Strategies and Skills for Children with Reading Difficulties*

Read-Aloud

Grade Levels: K–8

Description

All students need *models* of fluent and proficient reading. Silent reading is limited in this role. Although students can see their teachers or parents read silently, they can never hear or perceive what is happening while these models read. A *Read-Aloud* offers students the opportunity to "take a look inside" the reading of an expert and understand that, first and foremost, reading is language and should sound like it! Teachers' or parents' *oral* reading becomes the model that students strive to achieve.

When reading aloud to students, teachers model the kind of proficient reading that they would like their students to emulate. Thus, it is important that when teachers or others read to struggling readers, they practice the reading beforehand and feel confident that they can read the selection fluently. Indeed, to draw students' attention to the nature of the oral reading, teachers may wish to occasionally read with exaggerated fluency—adding a sense of the dramatic as they create different voices for different characters, pause dramatically, and vary the prosodic elements of pitch, volume, phrasing, and rate. Then, after the reading, teachers may spend a few minutes discussing the Read-Aloud with students, explaining the decisions they made regarding rate of reading, phrasing, and so forth, in order to communicate meaning.

Regardless of the student's age, fluent oral reading to the student, coupled with discussion of and response to the reading, should be a regular part of any instructional package for children who are struggling with reading.

Teaching Suggestions

1. Select a story, a poem, or another text to share with students. Choose a passage that you enjoy and one that you think students will enjoy. Books that have won awards or those on the International Reading

Association's Children's Choices (found in every October issue of *The Reading Teacher*) are good places to look for appropriate texts. Other references are listed in the suggested titles section, which follows. Stories are wonderful texts for reading aloud to students. However, students also need to hear other genres read aloud so that they can develop a sense for the many ways that texts are constructed. Poems, for example, often have a distinct pattern or rhythm. Nonfiction has its own unique structure as well.

2. Practice reading the text before sharing it with your students. Since one intent of the Read-Aloud is for students to develop a sense of what fluent oral reading sounds like, it is imperative that you read in a smooth and polished way—a presentation of the highest quality. Be sure to embed specific elements of expression into your presentation—increased and decreased volume, pitch of voice, voice changes to signal different characters, change in speed at appropriate places—all for the purpose of showing students how the reader interprets the author's intended meaning and conveys this to an audience. Of course, this will also increase students' satisfaction with the Read-Aloud experience.

3. Establish a regular time for the Read-Aloud. Try to make the physical environment comfortable and inviting for students. Allow students to sit on the floor if doing so is comfortable for them. It is also nice to have a carpeted area of the classroom for Read-Aloud experiences. A few pillows also add to the feeling that the Read-Aloud is something to be enjoyed and savored. You may wish to have a wooden rocking chair or other special piece of furniture from which to read. Indeed, that rocking chair can become the "reader's chair," where students sit when they read to the class. Lighting is another consideration for the environment. If possible, try to dim your overhead lights in order to create the appropriate mood for the Read-Aloud. You may want to set an end table next to your chair and place a table lamp on it.

4. Always indicate to students that they should listen for the meaning and the satisfaction that comes from a well-read story.

5. At the end of the reading, talk with students about the meaning of what they have just heard. What parts stood out for them, and

why? Do any parts need clarification? Did the story end the way they thought it would? Can they tell why you changed your voice and, if so, how doing so helped you to convey the author's intended message?

Suggested Titles

The references listed below offer a wealth of books that can be read aloud to children:

Title	Author (Last, First)	Publisher/Year ISBN
Best Books for Kids Who (Think They) Hate to Read: 125 Books That Will Turn Any Child into a Lifelong Reader	Backes, Laura	Crown/2001 9780761527558
Best Books for Children: Preschool Through Grade 6	Barr, Catherine	Libraries Unlimited/2006 9781591580850
Books to Grow With: A Guide to Using the Best Children's Fiction for Everyday Issues and Tough Challenges	Coon, Cheryl F.	Lutra Press/2004 9780974802572
Book Sense Best Children's Books: Favorites for All Ages Recommended by Independent Booksellers	Funke, Cornelia C.	Newmarket/2005 9781557046796
Best Books for Middle School and Junior High Readers: Supplement to the First Edition, Grades 6–9	Gillespie, John T.	Libraries Unlimited/2006 9781591584117
100 Best Books for Children: A Parent's Guide to Making the Right Choices for Your Young Reader, Toddler to Preteen	Silvey, Anita	Houghton Mifflin/2005 9780618618774
The Read-Aloud Handbook	Trelease, Jim	Penguin/2006 9780143037392

Teacher Voices

Gloria is a Title I teacher who reads to her students. Sometimes she works with students in their regular classrooms. At other times, she works with small groups of students in her own small classroom. She states,

> But regardless of where I am, I make it a point to try to read to all of the students every time I see them. It really sends an important message to these kids about what reading is and the enjoyment a reader or listener can get from a well-written text. But, you know, I read for another reason. I want them to hear how my voice can enhance their understanding and satisfaction of the reading. So many of my students are those who read in what I call a "defeated" sort of way. Their reading just drones on, even when they have had time to practice. These kids need to see that their comprehension will improve if they embed in their voice the intonation that makes reading come alive. When reading silently, these children will have an internal voice filled with expression and a joy for reading.

Extensions/Tips/Connections

Not all books need to be read in their entirety. You may wish to read only enough to get students hooked on the book. This allows students to make a direct transition from oral to silent reading, and it allows you to introduce your students to even more books throughout the school year. Having multiple copies of these books may be necessary, because several students will want to read the rest of the book to see how it ends.

Paired Reading

Grade Levels: 1–8

Description

Reading to students provides them with a model of how reading should sound. It is an indispensable part of any program to help students who struggle with reading and/or who suffer from negative attitudes about reading. However, reading to students is not enough. Students need plenty of opportunities to read on their own and opportunities to read with appropriate support and assistance.

Paired Reading is one of the most powerful ways to provide students with support. It is a one-to-one tutorial in which a struggling reader is paired with a proficient reader, such as the teacher, an older student, or even an age-level peer (Topping 1987). The two sit side by side and read one self-selected text together, with either the tutee or the tutor pointing to the text as it is read. Does it work? You bet! Topping reports that students made remarkable progress, accelerating both their comprehension and their word recognition when they read routinely with their parents. Similar results have been achieved when children work with other adults and students within the school.

Teaching Suggestions (based on Topping 1987)

1. At the first reading session, the student and tutor agree on meeting times.
2. The student chooses the reading material and can change it at any time. Remember that the tutor supports the reader while reading. This added support makes it possible for students to read just about any text of their choosing. Remember, too, that interest plays a big part in reading success. We are all more likely to stay with a text if we are truly interested in the topic.
3. Always begin by reading together. You may want to use a "1, 2, 3" signal so that you both know when to start.

4. Establish a signal that will indicate when the student wants to read solo. Most often this is a tap on the shoulder or a nod of the head. When the student signals to read solo, the tutor reinforces the student for taking the risk and continues to offer support throughout the solo reading. Both the tutor and the student may stop at logical points to talk about the meaning of what is read.

5. If a miscue is made, the tutor waits to see if the student self-corrects. If not, and the miscue alters meaning, the tutor points to the word and asks, "What would make sense here?" The student supplies the word or the tutor tells the student the word and resumes reading orally with the student, until the solo signal is again given.

With these suggestions in mind, then, the tutor explains how the procedure works: "Today when we read, we are going to read aloud together. When you feel that you want to read alone, remember to tap me on the shoulder and I will be silent. If you come to some words that you need to problem-solve, I will wait for you. If you have trouble solving the problem, I will help you by telling you the word and will continue reading aloud with you until you tap me out again." The two begin reading together.

Suggested Titles

Any text the student chooses to read is acceptable. Sometimes students will choose comics or newspapers, as well as books. Page 62 provides a list of references that can be used to locate good books for children.

Teacher Voices

Fourth-grade teacher Katherine has used Paired Reading for years and has developed a variation of it. In her words,

> We schedule an oral reading performance hour in our class on the last Friday morning of each month. I ask students to work with a practice partner, even though each child chooses his or her passage to read earlier in the month. The passage can be a poem, a selection from something the student has been reading for school or fun, or selections from great American speeches or documents, such as the Preamble to the

Constitution. Every student makes a copy of his passage and also receives a copy of his partner's passage, which he also practices. On the Tuesday, Wednesday, and Thursday before our Friday performance session, I give the students about fifteen minutes to work on their passages with their partners. Basically, each student reads along with his partner, providing help as necessary. Partners also discuss how to present the passage—as a duet or as a solo. This simple activity has improved all students' reading, especially those who find reading difficult and have a negative view of reading.

Extensions/Tips/Connections

Older struggling readers in upper elementary grades can become tutors for younger struggling readers in the lower elementary grades. The older student needs to be able to read the text selected by the younger reader so that she can provide assistance when needed; she also needs a lot of "good practice strategies"—what to do when the tutee comes to an unknown word. Both students benefit from the experience. In fact, some research has indicated that the older struggling reader makes the greatest gains (Topping 1989)!

Recorded Texts

Grade Levels: 1–5

Description

If Paired Reading appeals to you but you don't have enough volunteers to act as tutors in your classroom, don't worry. You can have your students listen to commercially produced tapes or CDs while reading. The use of *Recorded Texts* is based on the same theoretical foundation as Paired Reading: providing support via oral reading during the reading of connected text facilitates growth in reading. The key to the success of this strategy is that students listen to the oral rendition of a text while reading the same text simultaneously. Research has shown that this strategy enables students to increase their comprehension, overall fluency, and word identification abilities (Carbo 1978; Chomsky 1978).

Teaching Suggestions

1. Prepare short books, poems, or other texts by purchasing them or by reading them onto an audiotape or a CD. The recordings need to be read clearly and at an appropriate rate so that the reading sounds natural rather than contrived. Most commercial recordings signal readers when to turn the page. If you are making your own recordings, you will need to embed cues into the recording to alert readers when to turn pages.
2. Set up a regular time of day at which students can use the recorded versions. During the fifteen to thirty minutes devoted to this reading, show students how they are to listen and follow along in their texts. At the end of the reading, invite students to talk about what they read. If using a tape recorder, provide students with the recorder, tape, and headphones so that they can read along and others in the room will not be distracted. The same procedure applies to CDs, except, of course, you will need the CD player and disc.
3. For additional enjoyment and meaningful practice, encourage students to take the recorded versions and actual texts home.

Suggested Titles

Title	Author (Last, First) Read By (Last, First)	Publisher/Year ISBN	Suggested Grade Levels
Shipwreck at the Bottom of the World: The Extraordinary True Story of Shackleton and the Endurance	Armstrong, Jennifer Mali, Taylor	Audio Bookshelf/1998 1883332397	5–8
Duck for President	Cronin, Doreen Travis, Randy	Weston Woods/2004 0788205447	K–2
Because of Winn-Dixie	DiCamillo, Kate Jones, Cherry	Listening Library/2001 0807261866	2–4
The Neil Gaiman Audio Collection	Gaiman, Neil Gaiman, Neil	Harper Audio/2004 9780060732981	2–4
The Train They Call the City of New Orleans	Goodman, Steve Chapin, Tom	Live Oak Media/2005 9781581129042	1–3
Ida B.	Hannigan, Katherine Taylor, Lili	Listening Library/2004 9781400094837	4–6
I Stink	McMullan, Kate Richter, Andy	Weston Woods/2004 9780788203398	K–2
Bridge to Terabithia	Paterson, Katherine Leonard, Sean P.	Harper Children's Audio/2000 0694524522	5–7
Love from Your Friend Hannah	Skolsky, Mindy W. Hamilton, Laura	Listening Library/1999 080728078X	3–6
Charlotte's Web	White, E. B. White, E. B.	Listening Library/1991 0553470485	2–5

Teacher Voices

Some of Joe's third graders struggle with reading, and he has found that using Recorded Texts is an effective way to extend the students' reading beyond the classroom. Says Joe,

> My kids who have difficulty in reading really seem to like these recorded versions. They check them out to use at home. I have found that I need to provide "refresher minilessons" to remind students that they need to read the books while they listen to them. After students return the recorded version and text, I ask students to choose a brief passage within the text to read to me. Their improvement is obvious, as is their self-confidence. The real clincher is that I have seen this improved reading performance transfer to new passages that the students have never seen before!

Extensions/Tips/Connections

- Students can make Recorded Texts for all classmates, themselves, or students in lower grades. Making Recorded Texts is an excellent way to allow for individual differences, because different readers can prepare texts of varying difficulty. The key to success in preparing Recorded Texts is near-perfect reading. Much practice needs to occur before students actually record, and, even then, they may need to make more than one try. Here, again, is another meaningful way for students to practice reading. You may also want to invite the students to work in pairs or groups to prepare a recorded text. Featuring more than one voice can make the text even more enticing. This group recording is especially effective when students are recording stories that have several characters and much dialogue.
- The students at Jefferson Elementary have developed a cottage industry for recorded texts. It had humble beginnings, with a fifth-grade class preparing Recorded Texts for a second grade. The idea caught on, and soon all of the primary classrooms had intermediate classroom partners. Kindergarten and third grade, first grade and fourth grade, and second grade and fifth grade partnered. Some fifth-grade students took the idea a step further and produced texts through their school publishing company to sell to parents. (See Figure 4–2.)

First Grade Parents!

Help your children read with **Books on Tape**.

Andy and the Lion by James Daugherty (Trumpet)
Annabelle Swift, Kindergartner by Amy Schwartz (Trumpet)
Birthday Presents by Cynthia Rylant (Trumpet)
A Bug, a Bear, and a Boy at Home by David McPhail (Scholastic)
Frog and Toad All Year by Arnold Lobel (Scholastic)
Frog and Toad Are Friends by Arnold Lobel (Scholastic)
Frog and Toad Together by Arnold Lobel (Scholastic)
Hush Little Baby by Sylvia Long (Trumpet)
Little Bear by Maurice Sendak (Trumpet)
Sammy the Seal by Syd Hoff (Trumpet)
Somebody and the Three Blairs by Marilyn Tolhurst (Scholastic)
When the Fly Flew In by Lisa Westberg (Trumpet)

All tapes are $2.00. All tapes made with pride by fifth grade students of Jefferson Elementary.

Fill out the form below and return it to your child's teacher.

- -

BOT Publishing Company .... Jefferson Elementary

I would like to purchase the following tapes:

_____   Your name_____

_____   Child's name_____

_____   Child's teacher_____

All tapes are $2.00. Return this form to your child's teacher.

Figure 4–2. *Jefferson Elementary School's Books on Tape Order Form*

Listen to Children Read

Grade Levels: 1–5

Description

Sometimes it's a good idea for an adult to read to children. At other times, it's good for adults and children to read together. And at still other times, being a responsive, active, and enthusiastic listener is the appropriate role for the adult. In fact, researchers have discovered that listening to children read for as few as five to twenty minutes per day can have a powerful effect on their reading (Hewison and Tizard 1980).

Teaching Suggestions

1. Volunteers in the classroom, classmates, or students from different grades can easily listen to students read.
2. Provide time for readers to review the text to be read aloud to a listener. The rehearsal will help readers decide how to read the text aloud—what and where to place expression elements such as pitch, volume, rate, and pauses—to best convey the author's intended meaning.
3. Listeners need to show much patience and positive and sincere feedback during and after reading. Feedback can be general (e.g., "I like the way you read the whole story") or specific (e.g., "How did you decide to read this part with such expression?").

Suggested Titles

Title	Author (Last, First)	Publisher/Year ISBN	Suggested Grade Levels
Jazz: An American Saga	Collier, James	Holt/1997 9780805041217	4–8
The Girl Who Lived with the Bears	Goldin, Barbara	Harcourt/1997 9780152006846	2–4

Title	Author (Last, First)	Publisher/Year ISBN	Suggested Grade Levels
Beardream	Hobbs, Will	Atheneum/1997 9780689319730	2–4
Leon and Bob	James, Simon	Candlewick/1997 9781564029911	1–2
Rikki-Tikki-Tavi	Kipling, Rudyard	HarperCollins/1997 9780688143206	3–4
Butterfly Boy	Kroll, Virginia	Boyds Mills/1997 9781563973710	1–2
Lives of the Athletes	Krull, Kathleen	Harcourt/1997 9780152008062	3–6
Only a Pigeon	Kurtz, Jane and Christopher	Simon & Schuster/1997 9780689800771	3–5

Teacher Voices

Juan, a first-grade teacher, invites parents into the classroom to listen to children read. He comments, "My kids need a lot of opportunities to read, and they need interested listeners. Parents are always asking what they can do to help. Asking parents to listen to students helps me to accomplish both. What's more, listening is easy for parents, and the students look forward to reading to the adults."

Extensions/Tips/Connections

- Local celebrities can be enticed into being listeners. You may want to invite the mayor, town council members, school board members, and other leaders in the community to be listeners.
- Think about having a "read in" a couple of times each year. Students and listeners alike prepare and perform a favorite reading to share with others.

Fluency Development Lesson (FDL)

Grade Levels: 1–5

Description

Teachers who work with struggling readers may want to consider combining several different oral reading strategies to create even more powerful learning opportunities for students. The *Fluency Development Lesson* (FDL) is one way to do just that. It was developed and implemented with elementary-aged students by my colleagues and I [Tim] (Raskinski, Padak, Linek, and Sturtevant 1994). FDL is a combination of Read-Aloud, Choral Reading, Listening to Children Read, and reading performance and is implemented over an extended period. Normally it takes about fifteen minutes to implement with students when using poetry and other short texts (i.e., 100–200 words). The lesson is meant to supplement other reading experiences and is used at least four times weekly. The goal of FDL is to promote meaningful reading, fluency, and word recognition with students who need nurturing in one or more of these areas. During the lesson, the students listen to the teacher read a poem or other text to the class. Students then read the text chorally, pair up and practice reading the text with a classmate, and perform the text for an interested audience.

Teaching Suggestions

1. Prepare two copies of each text per child and teacher. The text is also put on an overhead transparency or chart paper and is usually a brief patterned poem or a portion of story that is often continued on following days.
2. Read the text to students several times while the students listen and follow along quietly on their own copy.
3. Discuss the meaning of the passage with the students. Also point out how reading with expression can enhance the meaning and how it makes others want to listen.

4. With teacher assistance, invite the class to chorally read the text several times. (See the section *Choral Reading* on page 51 for additional ways to engage students with this strategy.)

5. Pair the students with a partner. Each partner in each pair practices reading the text at least three times. The listener provides positive feedback (e.g., "I like how you read . . .") as well as help when needed.

6. Reconvene the class as a whole group. Invite some pairs to perform their texts for the rest of the class.

7. Ask students to choose three words from their text that they would like to include in their word banks. These words can be used for a variety of purposes, such as a spelling source for writing.

8. Ask students to put the copy of text that was used for the FDL into a folder for future reference or to take it home to read to their parents.

9. To prepare students for another interactive reading experience, begin the next FDL with a quick choral rereading of the previous day's text.

Suggested Titles

Title	Author (Last, First)	Publisher/Year ISBN	Suggested Grade Levels
The Important Book	Brown, Margaret W.	HarperCollins/1990 0064432270	1–3
Harvey Moon, Museum Boy	Cummings, Pat	HarperCollins/2008 9780060578619	K–3
Big Chickens Fly the Coop	Helakoski, Leslie	Dutton/2008 9780525479154	1–3
Arabella Miller's Tiny Caterpillar	Jarrett, Clare	Candlewick/2008 9780763636609	K–1
Pigs, Pigs, Pigs!	Newman, Leslea	Simon & Schuster/2003 0689849796	K–3
Rise the Moon	Spinelli, Eileen	Dial/2003 0803726015	1–3
Just a Minute	Watts, Irene	Chronicle/2003 0811837580	5–8

Title	Author (Last, First)	Publisher/Year ISBN	Suggested Grade Levels
Before John Was a Jazz Giant: A Song of John Coltrane	Weatherford, . Carole B	Holt/2008 9780805079944	K–2
Barefoot: Poems for Naked Feet	Weisburd, Stefi	Wordsong/2008 9781590783061	1–4
Roberto Clemente: Pride of the Pittsburgh Pirates	Winter, Jonah	Aladdin/2005 9781416950820	1–5

Teacher Voices

Second-grade teacher Marlene works with my colleague, Nancy Padak, and me [Tim] to implement the FDL in her classroom. Here's what she has to say about it: "Oh, it works, all right! Over the course of the year, students make significant progress in reading. Even though the formal research project has concluded, I am sold on the FDL and continue to use it. Research or not, I have seen students improve, and their growth is telling enough for me."

Extensions/Tips/Connections

Students learn a tremendous number of words from context. It is very important, then, to provide students with many opportunities to read authentic texts for authentic purposes. Another way of developing students' vocabulary consciousness is to have them select words from their texts to make personalized collections. Show students the many ways that words can be selected; for example, words can be chosen because of the way they sound when spoken or perhaps the way they feel on the tongue when they are pronounced. They can also be chosen based on unusual meanings or by the images they evoke. Providing students with time to share their word collections with one another is yet another way for them to expand their reading vocabulary and to see how words contribute to the richness of their lives.

CHAPTER 5

Guiding Assessment

O ne of the best ways to better understand how students approach reading is to observe and listen to them when they read. Recording their oral reading and carefully analyzing their miscues allow us to see the strategies they use in reading and those that need nurturing. We can design instruction that reflects our discoveries—instruction that will help all students reach their full reading potential.

We can also use records of performance to show students their own growth over time and to help students better understand themselves. This self-awareness is essential because it is the first step toward change. As Baker and Brown (1980) note, "If the child is aware of what is needed to perform effectively, then it is possible for him to take steps to meet the demands of a learning situation more adequately. If, however, the child is not aware of his own limitations as a learner or the complexity of the task at hand, then he can hardly be expected to take preventative actions in order to anticipate or recover from problems" (5). Becoming conscious of the strategies that they presently use in reading may, with teacher guidance, lead students to see that there are additional reading strategies they can learn. Once aware of these options, students can decide which reading strategies to use and when to use them to ensure comprehension. In other words, they can exercise control over their cognitive actions.

How to Use Oral Reading to Assess Reading

Perhaps one of the easiest and least intrusive ways to assess reading skill is to watch and listen to individual children read their self-selected books during independent reading time or during a personal reading conference with a child. You can use questions such as those in the following list to guide your general observations. You may also opt to record your informal observations on a card or in a notebook for future reference.

Suggested Questions to Guide Observations of Oral Reading

1. Does the student read for meaning?
2. What does the child do when meaning is not maintained?
3. Which cues—syntactic, semantic, and/or graphophonic—does the child use when an unknown word is encountered?
4. Is there any pattern to the child's miscues?
5. Does the child depend on the teacher or self when difficulties are encountered?
6. Does the student identify high-frequency words?
7. Does the reader read with a sense of meaning, expression, and fluency?
8. How well can the child recall or retell what was read?
9. Is the child willing to talk about the text with another person?
10. How does the reader perceive her own reading performance?

The What, Why, and How of Oral Reading Assessment Strategies

At other times, specific informal measures can be used to guide observations, providing ways to document what children do when they read. In any effective assessment strategy, three questions must be addressed:

- What do I want to know?
- Why do I want to know it?
- How can I best discover it?

Figure 5–1 shows how these three questions pertain to oral reading. Pages 89–99 provide directions for their use as well as reproducible

WHAT do I want to know?	WHY do I want to know?	HOW can I discover?
Does the student read for meaning?	Comprehension is the goal of reading. I need to know if the student is trying to make sense sense while reading.	Modified Miscue Analysis (see page 89) Multidimensional Fluency Scale (see page 96)
How does the student view his/her oral reading?	Change begins with awareness. Having children listen to and evaluate their own reading will help them become aware of how they sound when they read. Feeling more ownership in the process will make change more likely. I can help students set appropriate goals that will help them advance.	Student Self-Evaluation (see page 94) Retrospective Miscue Analysis (see page 93)
Does the student read with expression and fluency?	Fluency can affect reading comprehension. To best help my students, I need to know who is reading fluently and help those who are having difficulty.	Multidimensional Fluency Scale (see page 96)
How are the students' word-recognition skills?	Word recognition is one aspect of successful reading. Proficient readers use all three cueing systems. I need to know if the students are all using all three to ensure efficient reading.	Modified Miscue Analysis (see page 89)

Figure 5–1. *The What, Why, and How of Oral Reading Assessment*

assessment forms. Regardless of the strategy that is used, the following three principles remain constant.

Principle 1: Privacy

More often than not, students will be reading this text for the first time, which makes the reading hard enough! They don't need the pressure of performing for an audience at the same time. Here are three suggestions for ways to create privacy:

1. Pull students away from others one at a time to a designated area and have them read to you. This can be accomplished when students are completing other independent activities. It can also be accomplished when other students are reading a given selection silently. As the rest read to themselves, students can be pulled away individually to read a given segment.

2. Use a rolling chair. You might have a small room and therefore have no space to do "pull asides." Or perhaps you want your assessment to be as authentic as possible, so you decide to assess children while they are reading independently at their desks or tables. A rolling chair could be the answer. You simply roll from one student to the next and have each read aloud—loud enough only for you to hear. One teacher we know uses knee pads as a variation to this approach. He simply straps them on his knees and kneels next to children as they read, making his notes along the way.

3. Give the student an audiotape recorder and ask her to find a private spot and read the selected passage into the recorder. This approach provides children with the utmost privacy and allows you to work with other children while the child independently reads.

Principle 2: Observe the Child During the Reading

While the child reads from one copy of the text, make notations on another copy. Your notes can then be used for further analysis. You may also wish to use a tape recorder so that you can analyze, at a later time, the reading in greater depth. Taping the reading also enables you to focus all of your attention on the reader, answering questions such as those listed earlier. One additional advantage to taping is that you can replay the tape for the student. The student can then comment or answer questions about her own reading. These comments provide valuable insights for student and teacher alike. Like Strang (1969), we believe that students "seldom fail to show considerable insight" (81).

Principle 3: Trust Yourself

Rather than getting bogged down in miniscule procedures, remember that you are the expert here. Do what is necessary to best understand your students. If, for example, you want to determine whether a student's reading improves during a second repeated reading, have the student reread the text. Remember that you—rather than commercial or standardized tests—possess understanding about how students read because you use what you know about the reading process to help children become better readers every day of the school year. You see them read in different contexts throughout the school day. You see them interact with a variety of texts. You make informed decisions— decisions based on what you observe over time and contexts. Your observations are valid and reliable!

Procedures for Administering Informal Oral Reading Assessments

Modified Miscue Analysis

Miscue analysis was first developed by Kenneth Goodman (1969) as an alternative to traditional oral reading assessment that simply involved counting the errors students made while reading. Miscue analysis enables us to do an in-depth, qualitative assessment of the child's reading (Y. Goodman 1997); it attempts to determine which cue systems a student uses during reading (see Chapter 1 for an explanation of these cueing systems). Proficient readers use all cueing systems when they read. By determining those a student overuses or underuses, we can design instruction that helps the reader become more adept at orchestrating all cues in a way that enables easy and meaningful reading. In Clay's words (1979), "Teaching can then be likened to a conversation in which you listen to the speaker carefully before you reply."

Here is a version of miscue analysis that we have adapted for classroom use:

1. Choose an appropriate text. Although a formal miscue analysis requires 400 words or more, a passage of 150 words is acceptable for purposes of this assessment. The passage should be long enough to help you determine if and how the child uses different strategies. You may want to use passages from a commercial reading inventory or specific material that comes from your curricula. Make copies of the passage for you to write on and one from which the student will read.

2. Make copies of the Modified Miscue Analysis forms (Figures 5–2 and 5–3).

3. Explain the procedure to the child: "I would like to listen to you read so that I can hear what you do when you read. I am going to take notes as you read."

4. Watch the child as she reads. Do her body language or facial expressions note comfort or anxiety? Is she easily distracted? Does she hold the text at an appropriate distance from her eyes? Does she use her finger to point to the text?

5. As the child reads, make the following notations on your copy of the passage:
   - Circle any word that the child omits.
   - Add a caret (∧) for any word that the child inserts. Write the inserted word.
   - Draw a line through any word that is substituted. Write the substituted word.
   - Write a C on the word if the child self-corrects.
   - Note repetitions by writing R and drawing a line back to where the child repeats.
   - Draw slashes (//) between words to show how the child phrases.

6. After the reading, ask the child to retell what she remembers from the reading. How well does she recall the main events from the passage? Would you rate her recall as outstanding, adequate, or inadequate?

7. Analyze the child's reading using the Modified Miscue Analysis form (see Figure 5–2):
   - Write each miscue and the text that should have been read. Remember that self-corrects and repetitions are not counted as miscues.
   - For each miscue, ask the three questions on the form. If the answer is yes, circle the appropriate letter(s): M, S, V.

Reader's name _____ Grade _____

Title and Pages _____ Date _____

Three important questions to ask for each miscue:
M = meaning: Does the miscue make sense?
S = structure: Does the sentence sound right?
V = visual. Does the miscue resemble the printed word?

Student	Text	Cues Used
		M S V
		M S V
		M S V
		M S V
		M S V
		M S V
		M S V
		M S V
		M S V
		M S V
		M S V

Figure 5–2. *Modified Miscue Analysis Form*

© 2008 Michael F. Opitz and Timothy V. Rasinski, from *Good-bye Round Robin: 25 Effective Oral Reading Strategies, Updated Edition*. Portsmouth, NH: Heinemann.

1. What did the reader do when unknown words were encountered? (Check all that apply.)

_____ made an attempt in these ways:

___ used meaning cues   ___ used structure cues   ___ used letter-sound cues
___ made repeated tries   ___ used pictures   ___ skipped it and read on
___ used memory   ___ looked at another source
___ other: _____

_____ made no attempt   _____ asked for help   _____ waited for teacher help

2. Which cues did the reader use most often? _____
_____

3. How often did the reader attempt to self-correct when meaning was not maintained?
   (Circle one)   always   sometimes   seldom   never

Comments: _____

4. How often did the reader make repetitions? (Circle one)
                     always   sometimes   seldom   never

Comments: _____

5. Did the reader read fluently?   _____ mostly   _____ somewhat   _____ little

Comments: _____

6. Did the reader attend to punctuation?   _____ mostly   _____ somewhat   _____ little

Comments: _____

Comprehension

Retelling was (Circle one):   outstanding   adequate   inadequate

Comments: _____
_____

Other observations:

Figure 5–3. *Modified Miscue Analysis: Summary of Observations*

8. Answer all questions and record any additional observations on the Summary of Observations form (see Figure 5–3).
9. Based on your analysis, determine what you think the child needs to learn and choose appropriate instructional strategies.

Tip: Lynn Rhodes and Nancy Shanklin (1990) suggest another efficient way for busy teachers to complete miscue analysis, titled "Classroom Reading Miscue Assessment." Directions and a form are provided in the article, which is listed in the Works Cited at the end of this book.

Retrospective Miscue Analysis

First described by Yetta Goodman (1996), retrospective miscue analysis (RMA) invites children to become an integral part of the assessment process by reflecting on their reading. My own research (Opitz 1989) as well as that of several others has shown that children can share significant information that cannot be gleaned from other sources. Reflecting on their reading process informs us as teachers, but it also provides students with an opportunity to explore their own reading strategies, to better understand themselves. We have no choice but to recognize that children have something of value to report; when we are designing instruction, we must listen to them and use what they tell us. RMA is one method for accomplishing this. In addition to our analyses of the children's reading performances, students provide their analyses—which strategies they believe they used and how they monitored their reading to ensure comprehension.

Our adapted version of RMA uses these procedures:

1. After the child has read and retold a passage to you, return a copy of the passage to him and tell him that you are going to play back the recorded version of his reading. You want the child to listen to the reading while looking at the text.
2. Play back the recorded version. Stop the tape at certain points (usually when a miscue has occurred) and ask the child to talk about what he was doing at this place in the text. Yetta Goodman (1996) suggests the following possible questions. Of course, not all questions need to be asked about every miscue. Consider this list of

questions as a menu from which to choose rather than as a recipe that you must follow.

- Does this miscue make sense? Does it sound like the way we talk?
- Does the word in the text look like the word you said?
- (If the miscue was left uncorrected) Should you have corrected it?
- (If the miscue was corrected) How did you correct this miscue?
- Do you think this miscue affected your understanding? How?

RMAs can also be accomplished without a tape recorder; they can be done "on the fly" as a student is reading a text to you. Yetta Goodman calls these "critical teaching moments." When a student corrects a miscue during reading, you might ask, "How did you figure that one out?" or "Tell me about what you just did while you read." These critical teaching moments allow students to think more deeply about their own reading, reinforcing good reading strategies and leaving them in a position of knowing, so that they can become independent strategic readers, regardless of the type of reading they are doing—silent or oral.

Tip: If you want to know more about RMA, Yetta Goodman and Ann Marek (1996) provide a wealth of information and forms in their book *Retrospective Miscue Analysis: Revaluing Readers and Reading* (see Works Cited).

Student Self-Evaluation

Another way to invite students to reflect on their own reading is to use the Student Self-Evaluation guide (Figure 5–4). The following are some suggested ways to use it:

1. Once each month, ask students to read a passage into a tape recorder. Students then listen to their reading and respond to the statements on the form.
2. Provide students with time and a private space in which to complete this reading and reflection.
3. Ask students to share their evaluations with you, and ask them to state why they scored themselves the way they did.

Student Self-Evaluation

Name _____ Date _____

Title of Book _____

Pages read: _____

Directions:
1. Read each statement.
2. Check the appropriate column.

Statement	Wow!	Needs some work
1. I understood what I read.		
2. I tried to sound just like the character so others could understand how the character was feeling.		
3. I read smoothly so that my voice would sound just like the way it does when I talk with a friend.		
4. I read just right—not too fast and not too slow.		

I knew when I was running into trouble, and here's what I did:

_____

_____

_____

Figure 5–4. *Student Self-Evaluation Guide*

4. Use the results when designing instruction. For example, does more attention need to be given to comprehension? Perhaps what needs nurturing is reading with expression so that others will better understand the author's intended message.

Tip: Fourth-grade teacher Norbert uses computer software that allows his students to keep electronic portfolios. Students read directly into the computer and play back their recordings to hear how they read. Students save these readings in their electronic portfolios and use them to show their progress over time.

Given the attention that fluency has garnered in the last ten years, there are several new fluency software packages that enable students to practice reading orally, listen to their reading, select what they consider their best reading, and send it via the Internet to their teacher to hear and evaluate. Although this type of assessment ends with the teacher making some decisions about the reader, it begins with the student thereby enabling the student to become more thoughtful and self-reflective.

Multidimensional Fluency Scales

Effective oral reading is not simply a matter of getting the words right. Proficiency in oral reading is not marked word by word; rather, proficiency is determined by fluid or fluent reading in meaningful phrases and with appropriate expression that reflects the meaning of the passage. Just as a fluent speaker uses elements of oral expression—volume, pitch, rate, and pausing—to help the listener make sense of the message, so, too, does the fluent reader embed these elements to reflect and improve her own understanding of the text. Even when reading silently, the reader embeds these same elements in her inner voice to improve comprehension.

One way to assess readers' reading fluency is to listen to students read and assess their reading by using a rubric such as Figure 5–5. We recommend the following procedures:

1. Choose a passage or section of book. This could be the same reading used for the miscue analysis.

Multidimensional Fluency Scale

Student's name _____ Date _____

Text selection: _____

Directions: Use the scale in all three areas to rate reader fluency. Circle the number in each category that best corresponds to your observations.

Phrasing

1   Monotonic with little sense of phrase boundaries; frequent word-by-word reading

2   Frequent two- and three-word phrases, giving the impression of chopping reading; improper stress and intonation that fails to mark ends of sentences and clauses

3   Mixture of run-ons, midsentence pauses for breath, and possibly some choppiness; reasonable stress/intonation

4   Generally well phrased, mostly in clause and sentence units with adequate attention to expression

Smoothness

1   Frequent extended pauses, hesitations, false starts, sound-outs, repetitions, and/or multiple attempts

2   Several "rough spots" in text where extended pauses, hesitations, and so on are more frequent and disruptive

3   Occasional breaks in smoothness caused by difficulties with specific words and/or structures

4   Generally smooth reading with some breaks, but word and structure difficulties are resolved quickly, usually through self-correction

Pace

1   Slow and laborious

2   Moderately slow

3   Uneven mixture of fast and slow reading

4   Consistently conversational

Figure 5–5. *Multidimensional Fluency Scale (Zutell and Rasinski 1991)*

2. Make a copy of the passage for each student. You will make notations on these (i.e., teacher copies) as students read. However, you will have students read from the original (student copy).

3. Read through the Multidimensional Fluency Scale (Figure 5–5). This will help you determine what you are rating. Make a copy of this form for each student you intend to assess.

4. Show the passage to the student and allow him to practice reading the passage silently at least one time.

5. Ask the student to read the same passage orally. While he is reading, mark the phrasing by placing slashes (//) between the words to show how he chunks the text. You may want to write other observations as well.

6. After the reading, ask the student to tell what he remembers from the text. Then, based on your listening of his reading, use the recording sheet (Figure 5–5) to rate him on each dimension of the fluency scale by circling the number in front of the description that best describes how he read.

7. Attach the passage you marked (see item 5) to the fluency scale.

8. Interpret the results and design instruction accordingly. Activities for teaching specific skills are suggested throughout this book. An overview is provided in Chapter 1.

Reading Rate

Reading rate reflects only one small part of fluency. I [Michael] see reading fluency as the ability to silently or orally read a text with appropriate speed (adjusting to it as needed within a given text), relative accuracy, and appropriate phrasing, intonation, tempo, and expression (also referred to as *prosody*). Fluency is a dynamic rather than static process. Rate can sometimes indicate how well students process text. If readers encounter difficulties due to unfamiliar words or text structure, they will tend to slow down to give themselves time to fully analyze the text to ensure their comprehension of it. Slow, awkward reading also may be a sign that readers view reading as "getting the words" rather than understanding a message. Typically these children believe that they must say every word correctly in order to be proficient readers, yet nothing could be further from the truth! As

Goodman noted so many years ago (1969), "A reader who requires perfection in his reading will be a rather ineffective reader" (13). Efficient readers sample text, making predictions and confirming them along the way. When they realize that meaning has been lost, they do something to fix this problem. For example, they may reread. At other times, they may decide to continue, with the hope that subsequent text will help to clarify.

Assessing rate to create "speed readers" is a far cry from what we are advocating. Instead, we recommend seeing rate as one attribute of student reading. Focusing on reading meaningful text will develop efficient and effective readers. If anything, we want students to understand that they have to adjust their speed to their purpose for reading. Savoring the lines of a favorite quote, for example, calls for a different speed of reading than does skimming a text to locate a specific reference. With this explanation in mind, then, we offer the following formula to calculate reading rate:

$$\text{Rate in words per minute} = \frac{\text{Number of words in passage} \times 60}{\text{Number of seconds taken to read passage}}$$

We suggest that you determine students' reading rates on several different types of readings on several different occasions. Some reading researchers believe that children in given grades should read a given amount of words per minute (Raskinski and Padak 1996). However, remember that the last thing we want to do is confuse children by giving them the idea that fast reading is good reading. Comprehension is what matters!

CHAPTER 6

Involving Parents

O ral reading is not for school alone; it is perfect for home, too! In fact, researchers have discovered that parent and family involvement is a key ingredient that contributes to students' success in education in general (Henderson 1988) and reading in particular (Postlethwaite and Ross 1992). Students who read the most (both assigned and choice reading) tend to have the highest levels of reading achievement. All of this makes sense; after all, the reservoir of time most available for reading is at home, after school or during vacations—time that is under parents' control.

As in school, silent reading is the way students need to be reading at home. However, oral reading can play an important role in family reading experiences. During these family rituals, members use oral reading to share a favorite poem or an inspirational passage. Not only does oral reading provide a venue for children to share meaningful text with others, then, it also fosters emotional bonding among children, parents, and books. Indeed, when Holdaway (1979) conceived the Shared Book Experience (see page 48 for a detailed explanation), he was trying to recreate the atmosphere we use when we read to children at home. This chapter reviews ways that oral reading can be used at home with parents, siblings, and others.

Four Ways to Communicate with Parents

Regardless of the type of reading program envisioned for home involvement, good communication is an essential element. To best help children reach their full potential, teachers and parents (and students) must have established lines of communication. In many schools and classrooms, however, teachers and parents have little communicative interaction beyond that required through report cards and parent–teacher conferences. Many parents, overburdened with their own responsibilities, and perhaps haunted by memories of their own poor school experiences, avoid interactions with teachers. On the other hand, teachers may fear parents' unjustified criticism and attempts to tamper with the curricula. Teachers may feel that parents are unqualified to help their children in academic areas. And, very seldom are teachers taught how to work effectively with parents. The result? Often it is an unstated avoidance of one another.

Communicating with parents is a first step in establishing home–school connections. Fortunately, there are many ways that teachers can communicate: personal conferences, telephone conversations, e-mail messages, PTA meetings, and written notes. Following are four ways in which we can facilitate this communication.

Classroom Newsletter

Written communication allows for a poised presentation of information for parents and students alike; it serves as a reminder that literacy is used for genuine purposes in everyday lives. Creating a newsletter is one meaningful way to use written communication. What goes into a weekly, biweekly, or monthly classroom newsletter, particularly those that focus on children's literacy learning? Plenty! As Rick's newsletter shows (Figure 6–1), you can use this vehicle to let parents know about

- reading and writing activities at school
- specific ideas and instructions for helping children at home
- recently published books that might interest their children
- special reading and writing events
- author visits
- what their children have been learning
- student-selected poems
- announcements

The Room 12 Chronicle

Science
by Steven Bradshaw and Sammy Kart

For science the whole class was divided up into eight groups. Each group had a subject on the human body. For instance, muscular system, the five senses and more. Right now we are making notes and comments and after that we will give an oral report on what we studied.

P.E.
by Brennan Bird

This week we are doing a P.E. test with Ken our P.E. teacher. We will have to run a mile, do push-ups, trunk lifts, sit and reach and sit-ups. This will help us when we go to middle school P.E.. For some of us it will be kind of hard, but for some of us it will be easy. We we did some of this on Tuesday, May 5 around 10:20 AM.

Math
by Andrew Smith

In math the fifth graders are doing algebra, decimals, percents and geometry. The fourth graders are still working on fractions.

Art
by Eren Bilir

Recently in art we have been doing an art project called Combining Ideas. This is where we take all art techniques and put them on one piece of paper. For example, we have learned one point perspective, so we might take that and combine it with our regular drawing. They all turned out great. Another art project we have been working on is our Hand project. This is where we will trace our hands on a piece of graph paper and color each square differently. They look really nice too. We will be getting a new assignment soon.

Art #2
by Doug Tischer

Our most recent art project was titled "Stained Glass Drawing." For this activity we received a large piece of paper. With our pencils we drew squigly, straight and jagged lines reaching from one side of the paper to the other to make something like a jigsaw

puzzle. {This made some very interesting shapes.} Next, we took a black felt tip marker and went over the pencil lines. Then with oil pastels we colored each piece a different color, showing no white. The finished product looked like a piece of stained glass. Rick has stapled these up on the walls in our room. They all look very bright and colorful.

Reading
by P.J. Thompson

In reading we have just formed new reading groups. Reading group A is reading

Figure 6–1. *A Classroom Newsletter: The Room 12 Chronicle*

"Sarah Plain and Tall" Reading group B is reading "Charley Skedaddle" and last but not least Reading group C is reading "The True Confessions of Charlotte Doyle." All these books are in a different level of reading so the whole class can choose a different level of reading. I think all these books are very fun and interesting to read.

Writing
by Lynn Conell-Price

We have just finished writing thankyou letters to Malcolm Thompson and dpiX. In these letters we had a first paragraph thanking them for their efforts and generosity. In our second paragraph we told them everything we learned at dpiX. Then we wrote a third paragraph where we told them what we wanted to know, then we finished the letter with a sentence thanking them again for their generosity.

Weather Wise

You may know about the tornado in Sunnyvale that happened last Monday, well the the last tornado before Monday's storm that occurred in the Bay Area was in the east bay hills in 1952.

Weather Outlook

Friday: sunny
Temps:53-70 degrees F

Saturday: sunny
Temps:55-72 degrees F

Sunday: partly cloudy
Temps:53-69 degrees F

This copy of the Room 12 Chronicle has been edited by P.J. Thompson and Pre-read by Taylor Whitfield.

Geographical Roundup
Did you know California has the highest population in the United States.

Comics
by Keith Paul, Peter Jacobi, Alex Kerchoff and Alex Mamelok

comics on back

Figure 6–1. *Continued*

Of course, the newsletter is also an excellent place to publish students' writing. In fact, you can use the newsletter to teach children how to produce a literary publication. Once it is established, students take ownership by writing, publishing, and distributing it. It is but one example of how children can be engaged in an authentic, enjoyable literacy activity that mirrors what newspaper reporters do every day.

Explain How to Use the Newsletter at Home

We use the newsletter not only to share information with parents, but also to show parents how to use it as a springboard for many reading experiences at home. For example, parents can read aloud some parts of the newsletter and, if necessary, ask their children to clarify specific information. Children can read aloud other parts of the newsletter, providing concrete evidence of their reading growth. Here is what Barb, mother of Kelly, a fourth grader, has to say: "The newsletter is awesome. I often wonder how I can help Kelly at home. This newsletter answers my questions. I also like the different poems and suggested book titles because I want to keep reading interesting. I want Kelly to enjoy reading, and I am always on the lookout for good books."

Provide Parents with Some "Know How"

In previous chapters we explained several effective ways to use oral reading. Several of the strategies, such as Read-Aloud (see page 69), Paired Reading (see page 73), Recorded Texts (see page 76), and Listen to Children Read (see page 80), lend themselves to home use. To help parents and their children get the most from these activities, consider providing detailed instructions for a given strategy once every two weeks. You may include this in your newsletter, or you may decide to have a mini-inservice in the evening. If so, invite parents to bring their children. After you explain the strategy, invite the parents and children, with your guidance, to give it a try.

Invite Parents to Participate Both at School and Home

Frequently parents want to help, but they are not sure what to do or they feel that they are intruding on the teacher's territory. Emily,

Monica, and the Portage Elementary Staff provide three ways to issue invitations to parents.

Emily's Third Grade. From October through May, Emily asks her students' parents to read to them five days a week for twenty to thirty minutes each time. Emily assigns the first book to be read each month to provide busy parents with a fast way of choosing a book. She chooses a variety of books, making sure that they cross genres so that students become accustomed to a variety of text structures. *Tuck Everlasting* (fantasy), by Natalie Babbitt (1975), provides Emily's students with in-depth discussions at home and at school. Parents and their children read *Black Diamond: The Story of the Negro Baseball Leagues* (nonfiction), by Patricia and Frederick McKissack (1994), during March to celebrate the opening of baseball season. In May, students read *Pink and Say* (historical fiction), by Patricia Polacco (1994), in anticipation of Memorial Day.

Emily's class also celebrates Parent Reader Experience. Once every two weeks, a parent is invited to visit the classroom and read to the students. Emily occasionally recommends books to the parents, but they most often read a favorite story or a portion of a favorite story. If parents are a bit anxious about reading, they are invited to share with students how they use reading in their jobs rather than reading aloud to students.

Marcia's Fourth Grade. Marcia asks her students' parents to read aloud with their children, but each month she provides them with a different oral reading strategy.

> During October we start with parents reading to their children. November through March we emphasize Paired Reading [see page 73], Choral Reading [see page 51], and Recorded Texts [see page 76]. In April, parents are asked to listen to their children read [see page 80]. There's really no specific reason that these activities are used in specific months. I just want to make sure I vary the way parents interact with their children when reading to keep interest high. I make sure I explain the value and importance of the procedures. Although I didn't have any reason for the order of the strategies (other than variety), I have found that there is a

smooth flow from parents reading to their children in the first month, parents and children reading together in the middle months, and ending with parents listening to their children read. Parents and their children acquire many reading strategies that foster continued reading support and development.

Portage Elementary Staff. Teachers in Portage Elementary, a school located in a working-class neighborhood with a significant number of poor children, recognize the importance of parental involvement, reading aloud to children, early literacy experiences, and appropriate materials for parents to read to their children. As a service project, the school staff put together Mother Goose books that contained many short nursery rhymes. Their own classroom research informed them of the importance of phonemic awareness and how books with alliteration and rhyming could be used to help children develop it naturally. They also developed a pamphlet for parents that explained the importance of phonemic awareness, how to nurture it in naturalistic ways, and various activities parents could enjoy with their children.

The pamphlet and book were duplicated, and the pamphlet was inserted into the book. Now, several times each year, parents of preschool children are invited to the school for a ninety-minute session on immersing and engaging their children in reading. Each parent leaves the program with a copy of the Mother Goose book and much encouragement to read with their children.

Three Additional Ways to Connect Home and School

Following are three specific programs that are designed to heighten parental involvement. We present them as viable suggestions for busy parents who want to help their children read better.

Reading Millionaires Club

Informed teachers want to do everything they can to promote reading for pleasure and growth at home as well as at school. One program that capitalizes on this idea is called the "Reading Millionaires Club" (Baumann 1995; O'Masta and Wold 1991). The program begins with a calculation of the total number of minutes read if every child in the school or classroom reads twenty to thirty minutes every day after school. In many schools, this figure comes close to one million minutes, hence the name Reading Millionaires Club. The goal is to read one million minutes within seven or eight months.

Getting It Going. At the beginning of the school year, teachers make plans, draft forms, inform students and parents of the program, and plan a kickoff assembly for the event. At the initial schoolwide assembly, which also includes parents, children and teachers rally to get in the spirit of reading one million minutes during the next seven or eight months. Parents are told that they can use a variety of reading strategies with their children—reading to them, children reading to siblings, and paired reading, to name but three. Weekly forms are provided for each student. These forms are used to record the amount of time students read at home and the type of reading experiences. Students submit the completed form each Monday, and by the following Tuesday, ongoing statistics on the number of minutes read are reported by grade level and school. A thermometer chart, titled "Let's make reading hot at our school," is used to record the figures and is displayed in the hallway near the school entrance.

Keeping It Going. In addition to the tallying of reading minutes, periodic rallies, author visits, book fairs, reading festivals, and overnight read-ins, such as Friday Night Reading Special, are used to keep the reading ongoing. Students especially like the Friday Night Special because they get to bring their sleeping bags and blankets to the school library to "camp out" while reading.

Captioned Television

Captioned television appears to impact students' learning (Koskinen, Wilson, Gambrell, and Neuman 1993). When students watch television in which captions are displayed, their reading improves. As with Recorded Texts (see page 76), listening to the script on the television while reading it from captions has a reinforcing effect on students' word recognition and reading fluency.

Use this information to involve parents! Invite them to turn on the captioning feature (available on most television sets now sold in the United States) when their children are watching television. Parents should ensure that the volume is turned down several decibels so that children will have to take a close look at the text to make sense of the program.

Fast Start

Oral reading strategies can be combined to create lively, interactive reading experiences. Tim developed one and named it "Fast Start." He developed this strategy as a way to get primary-grade children off to a solid beginning in their formal literacy learning with the aid of supportive parent involvement (Rasinski 1995). However, the principles and ideas can be expanded to nearly any age or grade level. The key is to educate and support parents and to provide children and parents with texts that are interesting. The program is based on three sets of research findings:

- Parents reading aloud to children significantly benefits reading growth (Durkin 1966).
- Parents who read with their children in a supportive way, as in Paired Reading, can have a marked, positive effect on their children's growth in reading (Topping 1987).
- Parents who regularly listen to their children read can help them become better readers (Hewison and Tizard 1980).

In the Fast Start program, parents of primary-grade children are asked at the beginning of the school year to attend an orientation session in which the program and the importance of parent involvement are explained. Parents are informed that each month the teacher will send home packets of material for the parents to read to and with their children—one text every day, four or five nights each week. The texts are usually poems, some written by students and teachers. Others are favorites written by well-known poets. Because of poetry's brevity as well as rhyme, rhythm, and repetition of phrases and words, which makes them lively and predictable, they are an excellent choice for the program. Moreover, poems are meant to be read aloud. Much of the meaning of a poem is carried through the expression, volume, and phrasing that the reader brings to the reading. Thus, we feel that poems are ideal text for this sort of parental involvement. With younger children, we have used nursery and other rhymes that play with sounds. With older readers, we have selected more sophisticated poems as well as poems that are funny. Parents receive a newsletter that contains additional ideas. It also includes other literacy information, such as announcements of events at the local library and suggested books that students might enjoy receiving.

Following is a suggested sequence for engaging in a Fast Start activity that lasts from fifteen to twenty minutes each evening:

1. Read the poem, with expression, two or three times. Invite your child to view the text as you read.
2. Read the poem together with your children, again two or three times.
3. Talk about the meaning and your interpretations and insights into the poem.
4. Invite your children to read the poem to you once, twice, or three times. You may even wish to take different parts and perform the poem as a duet.
5. Take a look at interesting words in the poem. This word study could include finding, marking, and writing words that contain specific features.
6. Since you will be given several texts each month, feel free to return to old favorites and practice reading them.

Concluding Thoughts

Parent–child literacy experiences offer immeasurable support for children's development as lifelong and proficient readers. We heartily agree with Henderson's (1988) contention that "Parents are a school's best friend."

Authentic oral reading experiences enable parents and children to read together in ways that are enjoyable and satisfying and that foster reading growth. To reiterate, oral reading is not for school alone; it is perfect for home, too!

CHAPTER 7

Answering Questions About Oral Reading

You are not alone if you have some questions about oral reading. In this chapter we answer the most frequently asked questions about oral reading. Some questions may reflect yours; others may introduce you to aspects you have yet to consider. Each question and answer is of equal value; they are not listed in any particular order.

Where Did the Idea for Round Robin Reading Originate?

Researchers have yet to discover where the practice actually started (Hoffman 1987; Hoffman and Segel 1982). They have, however, made an educated guess based on their review of oral reading research. The story goes something like this: Around the turn of the century, educators relied on the story method to teach reading. This method included using literature, oral reading by the teacher (so that students could hear fluent reading), rehearsal of literature to be read aloud before others, and public performance. While this method was embraced by some, it was frowned upon by others who felt that learning individual words deserved greater emphasis. Gradually, words became the primary focus of teaching, and students were evaluated on their attempts to read words accurately during sight reading. Oral reading was the primary method used to check students' progress, and round robin oral reading was born (Hoffman 1987).

If Round Robin Reading Is So Detrimental to Children, Why Does It Persist?

Our own experiences as elementary teachers, our interactions with numerous teachers, and research on this topic have led us to formulate five primary reasons: tradition, classroom management, reading assessment, to save time, and not knowing what else to do.

Reason 1: Tradition. Our interactions with beginning teachers especially have helped us to understand the role tradition plays in round robin reading. New teachers learn about oral round robin reading as they observe other teachers, and, although they know several alternatives, they feel as though they would be "rocking the boat" should they break with tradition. Interviews with several veteran teachers confirm this view, which has remained constant for over two decades (Taubenheim and Christensen 1978). Most often they explain that they learned about the practice during student teaching and hesitated to give it up for fear of causing problems. They gradually came to believe that it didn't "hurt kids" and, therefore, continued the practice. As you have read, however, round robin reading can be harmful to students.

Reason 2: Classroom Management. Another reason we hear frequently centers on classroom management. Teachers tend to think that if they insist that all students do the same thing at the same time, they will be better able to manage and control student behaviors. While this reason may appear logical on the surface, a close examination of children who are expected to follow along reveals just the opposite. In fact, our observations have shown us that this practice actually can create more behavior problems than it solves. Many children become restless, especially if they are listening to a reader who is struggling to get through the text. The result? Students stray off task by either reading ahead, playing with their books, or becoming distracted. The teacher is forced to waste time trying to focus everyone and may feel quite annoyed and frustrated as a result.

Reason 3: Reading Assessment. As was discussed in Chapter 5, teachers use oral reading to assess a variety of reading behaviors. Asking students to read aloud in front of others appears to accomplish two purposes in one setting: (1) students read the story, and (2) teachers simultaneously assess students' reading. However, as discussed in Chapter 5, when teachers use oral reading for assessment, certain conditions must be in place, one of which is privacy. Reading material "cold" is hard enough without having to think about performing for an audience. In fact, it can cause learners to make more mistakes, invalidating any valid conclusions about their reading ability. If teachers use these results to design instruction for their students, they could inadvertently plan inappropriate instruction.

Reason 4: To Save Time. Teachers often feel pressured to require students to read an established number of stories. Therefore, skipping silent reading and asking students to read orally appears to save time. After reading the story orally one time, students can then progress to the next story. As discussed in Chapter 1, however, silent reading is actually faster than oral reading, so much time is saved when students engage in it. Further, research has shown that silent reading is more positively related to reading achievement (Armbruster and Wilkinson 1991).

Reason 5: Not Knowing What Else to Do. Well-intentioned, well-meaning teachers, such as those in the opening scenario of this book (see pages xvii and xviii), have shared with us that they rely on round robin reading because they do not know what else to do. Fortunately, as we present in this book, there are many alternatives. One important point to keep in mind, however, is that students should read silently much more than orally. When reading silently, all students are engaged. More often than not, this is not so during round robin reading.

My Students Don't Seem to Mind Round Robin Reading; in Fact, They Seem to Like It. Why Shouldn't I Use Something They Enjoy?

We want students to enjoy reading, and there are many ways that we can provide these enjoyable experiences. However, enjoyment alone is not enough. After all, children enjoy candy, too, but that doesn't mean that we let them devour it. Clearly, a child-centered classroom is not synonymous with a child-directed classroom. Using the most effective teaching strategies available, the teacher is responsible for facilitating the learning of *all* children. As stated earlier in this book, for example, we know that expecting all children to follow along in round robin reading can actually inhibit maximum reading growth rather than advance it (see Chapter 1). The teacher must use this knowledge when planning effective instruction that is advantageous to all. Children will adapt to the expectations.

When Will I Have Time to Assess Students If I Don't Use Round Robin Reading?

You can assess reading while students are reading silently. If students are reading silently in a small group, you can pull each student aside to read a given page to you. You can make notations about the reading the way you have in the past, and/or you can use some of our suggestions in Chapter 5.

Another way is to assess students during independent reading time. While they are engaged with their books, you can ask individual students to read to you. True, you may not be able to read with every student every day, but you can establish a schedule that will ensure that you will read with them every week. Make it your goal to listen to six students every day; by the end of the week, you will have covered your class.

At other times, such as at the end of a grading period, you may want to do a more complete assessment. For this, we recommend that you use the procedures and forms provided in Chapter 5.

Because I Have Used Round Robin Reading During Guided Reading for So Long That I'm a Little Afraid of Quitting "Cold Turkey," Do You Have Any Suggestions for How I Can Move Away from It Gradually?

Replacing one teaching strategy with another is risky business, primarily because we want to make sure students will learn as well, if not better, with the new strategy. Until we try it, we cannot be certain, but this is the only way we will ever know. Without question, replacing or augmenting yesterday's ideas takes much courage. Following are two ways to ease the transition.

Plan for Silent Reading. After building background and establishing purposes for reading in the "before reading" part of the lesson, invite children to silently read the entire story for the "during reading" phase of the lesson. Once all children have finished reading, have all but one student close their books. Ask that student to read a given portion and instruct the others to use the words to create pictures in their minds. This practice provides all children with opportunities to visualize, a skill that competent readers use when they read. When the reader is finished, ask her to hand the book to the next child and instruct that child to read. Continue this process until the students have finished reading the story.

Substitute Another More Purposeful Oral Reading Strategy for Round Robin Reading. For example, use Read to Discover (see page 39) to check students' understanding of a given text. Chapters 2 and 3 list several additional oral reading activities.

How Can I Be Sure That Students Have Read the Material If They Are Reading Silently?

Hold them accountable! Here are four ways:

- Invite students to read captivating stories. Reading interesting, well-written stories is perhaps the best way to ensure that students read. Students can't help but want to read stories such as these. (See the children's book section of the Works Cited for a starter list of children's books. Also note the references cited in Chapter 3 for additional books that will make reading a desirable activity.)
- Create a class or group discussion. Expect students to show understanding by their being able to discuss the material with others.
- Provide response logs. Response logs are notebooks in which students can write their ideas. Spiral notebooks are sometimes used, as are teacher-constructed notebooks (e.g., blank pieces of paper stapled between two pieces of construction paper). Provide students with a variety of tasks that enable them to show their understanding of the material. They might summarize a chapter, write three main ideas that correspond to the purpose for reading the selection, write a

character sketch, or complete a story map (i.e., a diagram that shows the elements of a story, such as characters, problem, and resolution).

- Use observation. After setting purposes for reading, you may decide that you want to sit and watch students read, providing assistance as needed. Your observations will reveal a tremendous amount of information about your students. Use the questions in Chapter 5 to guide your observations or use some of these: Which students appear to be so interested that they are reluctant to put down the book? Which students are able to read with minimal help? Who needs help, and what type of help do they need—understanding a section, identifying specific words? Which students appear eager to finish so that they can talk about the story?

If I Have Children Read Silently, Some Will Finish Before Others. Won't Those Who Finish Early Become Restless Waiting for Others to Finish?

True, students are like adults—they read at different rates and some will finish before others. This need not pose problems, however. In fact, it can create more learning opportunities. Consider the following options:

- If students are reading a story in a small-group setting, tell them before the reading actually begins that when they finish, they are to begin responding to the reading in writing. You may want them to identify and write responses to specific inquiries that were established prior to the reading experience. Were predictions accurate? What clues did the author use to help the reader solve the mystery?
- Again, if students are reading in a small group during guided reading time, tell students that they are to bring their independent reading book with them to the guided reading area. Once students have completed the assigned reading, they know that they are to read in their independent reading books until every member of their group has finished reading the assigned story. Discussion can then take place.
- If students are reading with less teacher direction, you can provide them with a variety of tasks to complete once they have silently read the assigned selection. These tasks can range from visiting the various literacy centers in the room to writing in their literature response logs in some manner.

Are There Ever Any Times When Having Children Follow Along While Another Reads Is Acceptable?

While round robin reading poses several problems, there are times when asking children to follow along while another reads is acceptable and desirable. Most often, following another's Read-Aloud combines silent and oral reading and is required for a specific purpose. Take fluency, for example. Perhaps you have some students who lack fluency, and you want the students to see and hear a fluent reader. In this case, you can provide the model by reading aloud while students follow your lead. You may also choose another student to model fluent reading. Several of the other oral reading activities mentioned in this book require that students follow the text while also reading aloud. These include those mentioned in Chapter 3—Readers Theatre, Choral Reading, and Shared Book Experience—and those mentioned in Chapter 4—Paired Reading and Fluency Development Lesson. Taped or CD stories and computer programs are still other ways that you can combine silent and oral reading to help students develop fluency and other reading skills and strategies.

What Should I Do When a Child Makes a Mistake (Miscues) When Reading Orally?

The answer to this question depends on your purpose for oral reading. If the purpose is for sharing and performing, help the child correct the miscue so that the sharing and performing can continue. If the purpose is for assessment, make notes about the miscue. You can analyze miscues to determine what type of help the child may need to advance as a reader. See Chapter 5 for ideas.

Can You Use a Combination of Oral Reading Ideas and Strategies?

Without a doubt! As with any good instruction, though, it is important to know why, when, and how to combine oral reading strategies. Say, for example, that you want to help all students develop fluency and comprehension while also creating a sense of community. After reviewing the many strategies explained in the previous chapters, you may decide to begin by inviting all students to read a selection silently.

You then proceed to pair them up and have them read to one another to provide them with some additional practice. Next, you decide to model fluent, expressive reading by reading aloud to them while they follow along. Last, you invite them to choral read the selection.

How Do I Respond to Colleagues Who Tell Me That Oral Reading Should Not Be Used?

Our guess is that when colleagues talk about not using oral reading, they are most likely speaking of round robin reading. If this is so, we agree with them for reasons presented earlier in this book (see Chapter 1). If they are talking about all oral reading, we disagree. We have presented a rationale for using oral reading as well as specific activities that foster proficient reading. Perhaps you can use both to show your colleagues that there are times when oral reading can be advantageous.

Is There a Balance I Should Achieve with Oral and Silent Reading?

Not really. You will rely on silent reading because it is ultimately a faster mode of reading and it best represents how readers read most often. Silent reading is more positively related to reading gains than is small-group oral reading. We use oral reading for specific purposes, such as those stated in Chapter 1.

And, as Artley (1972) says, "If no good purpose exists, if the others in the group already know what the writer has said, then there is no occasion for oral reading. There is no rule in the book that says that every child must read aloud every day" (49). Artley also reminds us that silent reading is really the foundation of oral reading; that is, readers reconstruct the writer's ideas and sense the feeling of the text during silent reading. These are then conveyed to interested listeners via oral reading.

Is There a Certain Grade Level at Which Oral Reading Should End?

No. Oral reading is often more prevalent in the first and second grade because of the many shared reading experiences that teachers use to help children become readers. It is also used more often because silent reading is a language process and behavior that is learned over time. When teaching first grade, Michael had to teach students what it meant to read silently. This usually progressed from reading aloud to oneself to whispering to moving lips to internalized reading that could not be heard. However, there are times throughout one's schooling, college, and life experiences when oral reading is appropriate. Michael recently attended an award ceremony, for example, during which the individual presenting the awards read aloud a short statement explaining the award winner's contributions. Again, we return to purpose. Why might a fifth-grade teacher ask his students to read aloud? Perhaps he wants his students to share or perform their reading. Perhaps he wants to assess their reading. Again, actions are guided by purpose.

More Recommended Children's Literature by Strategy

Think-Aloud

Crowe, C. 2008. *Turtle Girl*. Honesdale, PA: Boyds Mills.

Diakite, B. W. 2003. *The Magic Gourd*. New York: Scholastic.

Hoyt-Goldsmith, D. 1997. *Potlatch: A Tsimshian Celebration*. New York: Holiday House.

Kramer, S. P. 1999. *Eye of the Storm*. New York: Penguin.

Lester, J. 2003. *Shining*. Orlando, FL: Harcourt.

Rucki, A. 1998. *When the Earth Wakes*. New York: Scholastic.

Trueman, T. 2008. *Hurricane*. New York: HarperCollins.

Turtle, E. W. 1997. *Full Moon Stories: Thirteen Native American Stories*. New York: Hyperion.

Induced Imagery

Banks, K. 2008. *Max's Dragon*. New York: Farrar, Straus & Giroux.

Bernhard, E. 1997. *Prairie Dogs*. Orlando, FL: Harcourt.

Cleary, B. 2000. *Dear Mr. Henshaw*. New York: HarperCollins.

Golding, T. M. 2008. *Niner*. Asheville, NC: Front Street.

Hiscock, B. 2008. *Ookpik: The Travels of a Snow Owl*. Honesdale, PA: Boyds Mills.

Wardlaw, L. 1997. *Punia and the King of Sharks*. New York: Dial.

Wheeler, L. 2003. *One Dark Night*. San Diego, CA: Harcourt.

Directed Listening Thinking Activity (DLTA)

Ada, A. F. 1998. *The Malachite Palace*. New York: Atheneum.

Borden, L. 1998. *Good-Bye Charles Lindbergh*. New York: Simon & Schuster.

Bunting, E. 2008. *Mouse Island*. Honesdale, PA: Boyds Mills.

Chichester, E. C. 2003. *Follow the Leader*. New York: Margaret K. McElderry Books.

Christelow, E. 2003. *Vote!* New York: Clarion.

Cronin, D. 2004. *Duck for President.* New York: Atheneum.

England, L. 1998. *The Old Cotton Blues.* New York: Margaret K. McElderry Books.

Feldman, J. 2008. *The Golly Whopper Games.* New York: Greenwillow.

Frost, H. 2008. *Monarch and Milkweed.* New York: Atheneum.

Glassman, P. 2003. *My Dad's Job.* New York: Simon & Schuster.

Isadora, R. 2008. *The Fisherman and His Wife.* New York: G. P. Putnam's Sons.

Janulewicz, M. 1997. *Yikes! Your Body, Up Close!* New York: Simon & Schuster.

Munsch, R. 2003. *Lighthouse: A Story of Remembrance.* New York: Scholastic/Cartwheel Books.

Nivola, C. 2008. *Planting the Trees of Kenya.* New York: Farrar, Straus & Giroux.

Thomas, P. 2008. *Farmer George Plants a Nation.* Honesdale, PA: Calkins Creek.

Look for the Signals

Adler, D. A. 1998. *Chanukay in Chelm.* New York: HarperCollins.

Appelt, K. 1996. *Watermelon Day.* New York: Macmillan.

Borton, L. 1997. *Junk Pile!* New York: Philomel.

Goldfinger, J. P. 2007. *My Dog Lyle.* New York: Clarion.

Lakin, P. 2007. *Rainy Day.* New York: Dial.

Lewis, J. P. 1997. *The La-Di-Da Hare.* New York: Atheneum.

Lobel, A. 2008. *Hello, Day!* New York: Greenwillow.

Mayer, B. 2008. *All Aboard!* New York: Margaret K. McElderry Books.

Plourde, L. 2008. *Science Fair Day.* New York: Dutton.

Rogers, P. 1996. *Cat's Kittens.* New York: Viking

Shipton, J. 1999. *What If?* New York: Dial.

Stainton, S. 2007. *I Love Cats.* New York: Katherine Tegen Books

Willis, J. 2005. *Gorilla! Gorilla!* New York: Atheneum.

Wong, J. S. 2007. *The Dumpster Diver.* Cambridge, MA: Candlewick.

Say It Like the Character

Bluthenthal, D. C. 2003. *I'm Not Invited.* New York: Atheneum.

Bottner, B. 2003. *The Scaredy Cats.* New York: Simon & Schuster.

Dewdney, A. 2007. *Llama, Llama Mad at Mama.* New York: Viking.

Graff, L. 2008. *The Life and Crimes of Bernetta Wallflower.* New York: Laura Geringer Books.

Kuskin, K. 2005. *So, What's It Like to Be a Cat?* New York: Atheneum.

Littlesugar, A. 1997. *Jonkonnu.* New York: Philomel.

McGhee, A. 2004. *Mrs. Watson Wants Your Teeth*. Orlando, FL: Voyager.

Shepard, A. 1998. *The Crystal Heart: A Vietnamese Legend*. New York: Atheneum.

Skarmeta, A. 2003. *The Composition*. Toronto, ON: Groundwood Books.

Thompson, K. 2005. *Eloise: The Absolutely Essential 50th Anniversary Edition*. New York: Simon & Schuster.

Rapid Retrieval of Information (RRI)

Aronson, M. 2007. *Up Close: Robert F. Kennedy*. New York: Puffin.

Gibbons, G. 2007. *Snakes*. New York: Holiday House.

Horenstein, H. 1997. *Baseball in the Barrios*. Orlando, FL: Gulliver.

Hoyt-Goldsmith, D. 2008. *Cinco de Mayo, Celebrating the Traditions of Mexico*. New York: Holiday House.

Hurmence, B. 1997. *Slavery Time: When I Was Chillun*. New York: Putnam.

Lewin, T. 2003. *Lost City: The Discovery of Machu Picchu*. New York: Philomel.

Pringle, L. 2008. *Sharks! Strange and Wonderful*. Honesdale, PA: Boyds Mills.

Robinet, H. G. 1997. *The Twins, the Pirates, and the Battle of New Orleans*. New York: Simon & Schuster.

Seidensticker, J. 2008. *Predators*. New York: Simon & Schuster.

Urbigkit, C. 2008. *The Shepherd's Trail*. Honesdale, PA: Boyds Mills.

Vanasse, D. 2004. *The Distant Enemy*. Anchorage, AK: Todd Communications.

Read to Discover

Ashman, L. 2003. *Rub-a-Dub Sub*. Orlando, FL: Harcourt.

Fitzgibbon, M. 2008. *Amazing Wonders Collection: Tyrannosaur*. Cambridge, MA: Candlewick.

George, L. B. 2005. *The Secret*. New York: Greenwillow.

Hamilton, L. 2008. *Horse: The Essential Guide for Young Equestrians*. Cambridge, MA: Candlewick.

Suen, A. 2003. *Raise the Roof!* New York: Viking.

Swanson, S. M. 2008. *To Be Like the Sun*. Orlando, FL: Harcourt.

Walsh, J. P. 1997. *When I Was Little Like You*. New York: Viking.

Revised Radio Reading

Eaton, J. C. 2008. *The Facttracker*. New York: HarperCollins.

Evans, D. 2004. *MVP: Magellan Voyage Project*. Honesdale, PA: Front Street.

Shared Book Experience

Busby, A. 2003. *Drat That Fat Cat!* London: Arthur Levine.
Horacek, P. 2007. *Butterfly, Butterfly*. Cambridge, MA: Candlewick.
Kimmel, E. C. 2003. *What Do You Dream?* Cambridge, MA: Candlewick.
Merz, J. J. 2007. *Playground Day!* New York: Clarion.
Steggall, S. 2008. *The Life of a Car*. New York: Holt.
Wilson, K. 2008. *Hilda Must Be Dancing*. New York: Aladdin.

Choral Reading

Baker, K. 2007. *Hickory Dickory Dock*. Orlando, FL: Harcourt.
Baker, K. 2008. *Potato Joe*. Orlando, FL: Harcourt.
Barrett, J. 2008. *Never Take a Shark to the Dentist and Other Things Not to Do*. New York: Atheneum.
Berry, L. 2008. *Duck Dunks*. New York: Holt.
Birney, B. 1996. *Pie's in the Oven*. New York: Houghton Mifflin.
Emmett, J. 2006. *She'll Be Coming Round the Mountain*. New York: Atheneum.
Grossnickle, A. H. 2008. *One, Two, Buckle My Shoe*. Orlando, FL: Harcourt.
Rodda, E. 1997. *Yay!* New York: Greenwillow.
Rylant, C. 2008. *Puppies and Piggies*. Orlando, FL: Harcourt.

Readers Theatre

George, L. B. 2006. *In the Garden: Who's Been Here?* New York: Greenwillow.
Hall, D. 1994. *I Am the Dog, I Am the Cat*. New York: Dial.
Johnson, A. 1989. *Tell Me a Story, Mama*. New York: Scholastic.
Lobel, A. 1983. *Fables*. New York: HarperCollins.
Raschka, C. 2007. *Yo! Yes?* New York: Scholastic.
Urbanovic, J. 2008. *Duck Soup*. New York: HarperCollins.

Poetry Club

Asch, F. 1996. *Sawgrass Poems*. Orlando, FL: Harcourt Brace.
Branwell, Y. M. 2008. *We Are One*. Orlando, FL: Harcourt.
Cheng, A. 2008. *Where the Steps Were*. Honesdale, PA: Wordsong.
Dakos, K. 1990. *If You're Not Here, Please Raise Your Hand*. New York: Simon & Schuster.
De Fina, A. 1997. *When a City Leans Against the Sky*. Honesdale, PA: Wordsong.

Fleischman, P. 1989. *I Am Phoenix: Poems for Two Voices*. New York: HarperCollins.

Florian, D. 1996. *On the Wing*. Orlando, FL: Harcourt Brace.

Florian, D. 1997. *In the Swim*. Orlando, FL: Harcourt.

Herrick, S. 2005. *Naked Bunyip Dancing*. Asheville, NC: Front Street.

Hopkins, L. B. 1996. *School Supplies*. New York: Simon & Schuster.

Hughes, L. 1994. *The Dream Keeper and Other Poems*. New York: Scholastic.

Johnston, T. 1996. *Once in the Country*. New York: Putnam.

Lawson, J. A. 2006. *Black Stars in a White Night Sky*. Honesdale, PA: Wordsong.

Robb, L. 1997. *Music and Drum*. New York: Philomel.

Singer, M. 2003. *Fireflies at Midnight*. New York: Atheneum.

VanWassenhove, S. 2008. *The Seldom-Ever Shady Glades*. Honesdale, PA: Wordsong.

Vestergaard, H. 2007. *I Don't Want to Clean My Room: A Mess of Poems About Chores*. New York: Dutton.

Yolen, J. 1995. *Alphabestiary: Animal Poems from A to Z*. New York: St. Martin's.

Recorded Texts

Danziger, P. 1997. *The Amber Brown Collection*. Read by A. Witt. Westminster, MD: Listening Library.

Davies, N. 2008. *Bat Loves the Night*. Cambridge, MA: Candlewick.

Davies, N. 2008. *Big Blue Whale*. Cambridge, MA: Candlewick.

Davies, N. 2008. *One Tiny Turtle*. Cambridge, MA: Candlewick.

Davies, N. 2008. *Surprising Sharks*. Cambridge, MA: Candlewick.

French, V. 2008. *Growing Frogs*. Cambridge, MA: Candlewick.

Gleitzman, M. 2004. *Girl Underground*. Read by M.-A. Fahey. Victoria, Australia: Bolinda Audio.

Hansard, P. 2008. *A Field Full of Horses*. Cambridge, MA: Candlewick.

Osborne, M. P. 2000. *The Magic Treehouse Collection*. Read by M. P. Osborne. New York: Imagination Studio.

Snicket, L. 2004. *The Bad Beginning: A Series of Unfortunate Events*, Book the First. Read by T. Curry. Westminster, MD: Listening Library.

Fluency Development Lesson (FDL)

Calmenson, S. 2008. *Jazzmatazz!* New York: HarperCollins.

Cameron, A. 1989. *The Stories Julian Tells*. New York: Random House.

Ireland, K. 2003. *Don't Take Your Snake for a Stroll*. San Diego, CA: Harcourt.

Snow, A. 2007. *The Snack Smasher and Other Reasons It's Not My Fault*. New York: Atheneum.

Appendix B

Recommended Websites by Strategy

Rapid Retrieval of Information/R[...]over

www.eduhoundsitesets.com

Eduhound Site Sets provides an [...] c-based online resources for educators to impl[...] website links are often linked to Time for Kid[...] provide supplemental activities that would u[...] se of the rapid retrieval of information strategy.

www.ipl.org/div/kidspace

Kidspace at The Internet Public Library offers a well-organized collection of resources sorted by topic. These sites provide many opportunities for students to explore and for teachers to integrate informational texts into a variety of content reading lessons.

Readers Theatre/Choral Reading

www.aaronshep.com

Aaron Shepard's Home Page offers a variety of scripts, tips, and other resources for teachers and families to instill a dramatic passion for reading through storytelling, authoring, and sharing literacy in many ways. Although the majority of the site had been focused in readers theatre, Shepard has branched out into other avenues of catching the attention of all ages through interpretive read-aloud.

Poetry Club

www.poetry4kids.com

Kenn Nesbitt's Children's Poetry Playground provides a number of opportunities for kids to enjoy written poetry and poems read aloud by the author through the use of podcasts. In addition, this site has several features, such as games, tips, places to publish, and rhyming dictionaries, offering support and encouragement to kids writing their own poetry.

www.poetryarchive.org

The Poetry Archive boasts a very impressive and well-organized collection of historic and current recordings of poets reading their own works. This site has a separate yet linked site especially for elementary-aged children with poets such as Roald Dahl, Valerie Bloom, and Michael Rosen enthusiastically sharing their work. Teachers, librarians, parents, and kids will enjoy reading a myriad of poems and biographies of the poets, listening to the authors as they share their interpretations of their own works, as well as viewing and listening to interviews with the poets themselves.

Read-Aloud/Read Around

www.childrenslibrary.org

International Children's Digital Library: A Library for the World's Children offers access to thousands of digital texts from more than 45 different cultures through a very easy-to-use interface in which users can search for texts by type, language, age range, publication dates, and other parameters. This site will be of interest to educators of English language learners and students of all ages as it provides opportunities to connect with the global and historical aspects of literature. Students, teachers, and parents from a variety of backgrounds will find texts they are eager to share through reading aloud or reading around!

www.storylineonline.net

Storyline Online is an online streaming video program featuring members of the Screen Actors Guild reading children's books aloud. Actors and actresses known to both children and adults, including Sean Astin, Elijah Wood, and Jason Alexander among many others, combine their love of reading and talents in acting to provide viewers with delightful experiences listening and viewing favorites like *A Bad Case of Stripes* by David Shannon, *Thank You, Mr. Falker* by Patricia Polacco, and many others.

www.bookwink.com

Bookwink, a site devoted to inspiring kids in the third to eighth grade to find their reading interests, provides podcast book talks and an annotated, easy-to-navigate bibliography of texts appropriate for readers in this age bracket. Given that this is a crucial age to impact lifelong reading, this student-friendly site has much to offer in its clear and focused design.

Multiple Strategies

www.readwritethink.org

Read, Write, Think provides educators and students access to high-quality practices and resources in reading and language arts instruction. Developed by the International Reading Association in conjunction with the National Council of Teachers of English, this website has a lengthy list of web-based resources and a variety of lesson plans with linked activities organized by grade level and covering topics such as reading aloud, partner reading, fluency development, shared reading, readers theatre, and many others. Many lessons emphasize the cross-curricular nature of reading instruction and use of reading strategies.

www.readingrockets.org

Reading Rockets offers a wealth of information about reading strategies, lessons, and activities designed to help young children learn how to read and read better. These reading resources assist parents, teachers, and other educators in working with struggling readers who require additional help in reading fundamentals and comprehension skills development. These resources take on a variety of forms including PBS television specials provided online with video streaming, podcasts, webcasts, links to research articles, guides to find appropriate children's literature, current events in reading, and hundreds of other useful and well-organized links for educators and families.

www.busyteacherscafe.com/unit.htm

Busy Teacher's Café Theme Units, Lessons, and Activities is an area of the online café in which teachers are provided overviews in concepts such as readers theatre and fluency development. Along with this information, the plentiful list of links provided through these theme units lead teachers to sites providing online read-alouds, readers theatre scripts developed from popular children's literature, rubrics for a variety of oral reading assessment purposes, and reusable lesson plan templates.

www.scholastic.com

Scholastic has expanded their involvement in children's literacy beyond the publishing of great children's literature to supporting children, teachers, and parents in developing lifelong readers of all ages. This site is very well organized, with divisions of resources into three categories: teachers, parents, and kids. Of greatest interest in applying effective oral reading practices are the tips and research supporting the read-aloud techniques of parents and teachers. In addition, the BookFlix program in which fiction and nonfiction texts are paired by theme and read aloud with highlighted captioning and linked activities provides a unique opportunity for students to compare and contrast fiction and nonfiction texts while easily accessing text at various levels. Finally, teachers and parents will find articles, lessons, and activities involving readers theatre, poetry, recorded texts, and fluency development.

Works Cited

Professional Works

Allington, R. 1980. "Teacher Interruption Behaviors During Primary Grade Oral Reading." *Journal of Educational Psychology* 72: 371–372.

———. 1984. "Oral Reading." In *Handbook of Reading Research*. Eds. R. Barr, M. Kamil, and P. Mosenthal. New York: Longman.

Anderson, R., E. Hiebert, I. Scott, and I. Wilkinson. 1985. *Becoming a Nation of Readers: The Report of the Commission on Reading.* Washington, DC: National Institute of Education.

Anderson, R., P. Wilson, and L. Fielding. 1988. "Growth in Reading and How Children Spend Their Time Outside of School." *Reading Research Quarterly* 23: 285–303.

Armbruster, B., and I. Wilkinson. 1991. "Silent Reading, Oral Reading, and Learning from Text." *The Reading Teacher* 45: 154–155.

Artley, A. S. 1972. "Oral Reading as a Communication Process." *The Reading Teacher* 26: 46–51.

Baker, L., and A. Brown. 1980. *Metacognitive Skills and Reading.* (Technical Report No. 188). Urbana, IL: University of Illinois, Center for the Study of Reading. (ERIC Document Reproduction Service No. 195 932).

Barchers, S. 1993. *Readers Theatre for Beginning Readers.* Englewood, CO: Teacher Ideals Press.

Barrera, R., V. Thompson, and M. Dressman, eds. 1997. *Kaleidoscope: A Multicultural Booklist for Grades K–8.* 2d ed. Urbana, IL: National Council of Teachers of English.

Baumann, N. 1995. "Reading Millionaires—It Works!" *The Reading Teacher* 48: 730.

Block, C. 1997. *Literacy Difficulties: Diagnosis and Instruction.* San Diego: Harcourt Brace.

Braun, W., and C. Braun. 1996. *A Readers Theatre Treasury of Stories.* Calgary, Alberta: Braun and Braun Associates.

Butler, D. 1985. *Babies Need Books.* New York: Atheneum.

Carbo, M. 1978. "Teaching Reading with Talking Books." *The Reading Teacher* 32: 267–273.

Children's Choices. 1995. *More Kids' Favorite Books.* Newark, DE: International Reading Association.

Chomsky, C. 1978. "When You Still Can't Read in Third Grade: After Decoding, What?" In *What Research Has to Say About Reading Instruction.* Ed. S. Samuels. Newark, DE: International Reading Association.

Clay, M. 1979. *The Early Detection of Reading Difficulties.* 3d ed. Portsmouth, NH: Heinemann.

Daneman, M. 1991. "Individual Differences in Reading Skills." In *Handbook of Reading Research, Volume 2.* Eds. R. Barr, M. Kamill, P. Mosenthal, and P. D. Pearson. White Plains, NY: Longman.

Davey, B. 1983. "Think Aloud—Modeling the Cognitive Processes of Reading Comprehension." *Journal of Reading* 27: 44–47.

Dixon, N., A. Davies, and C. Politano. 1996. *Learning with Readers Theatre.* Winnipeg, Canada: Peguin.

Doiron, R. 1994. "Using Nonfiction in a Read-Aloud Program: Letting the Facts Speak for Themselves." *The Reading Teacher* 47: 616–624.

Dole, I., G. Duffy, L. Roehler, and P. D. Pearson. 1991. "Moving from the Old to the New: Research on Reading Comprehension Instruction." *Review of Educational Research* 61: 239–264.

Durkin, D. 1966. *Children Who Read Early.* New York: Teachers College Press.
———. 1993. *Teaching Them to Read.* 6th ed. Needham Heights, MA: Allyn and Bacon.

Elley, W. 1989. "Vocabulary Acquisition from Listening." *Reading Research Quarterly* 24: 174–187.

Fowler, J., and S. Newlon. 1995. *Quick and Creative Literature Response Activities.* New York: Scholastic.

Fredericks, A. 1993. *Frantic Frogs and Other Frankly Fractured Folktales for Readers Theatre.* Westport, CT: Teacher Ideas Press.

Freeman, J. 1997. *More Books Kids Will Sit Still For.* New York: Bowker.

Freire, P. 1985. "Reading the World and Reading the Word: An Interview with Paulo Friere." *Language Arts* 62: 15–21.

Gambrell, L., and P. Jawitz. 1993. "Mental Imagery, Text Illustrations, and Children's Story Comprehension and Recall." *Reading Research Quarterly* 28: 265–276.

Gambrell, L., B. Kapinus, and R. Wilson. 1987. "Using Mental Imagery and Summarization to Achieve Independence in Comprehension." *Journal of Reading* 30: 638–642.

Gillespie, J., and C. Gilbert, eds. 1985. *Best Books for Children: Preschool Through the Middle Grades*. New York: Bowker.

Gillet, J., and C. Temple. 1994. *Understanding Reading Problems: Assessment and Instruction*. 4th ed. New York: HarperCollins.

Goodman, K. 1965. "A Linguistic Study of Cues and Miscues in Reading." *Elementary English* 42: 633–643.

———. 1969. *Analysis of Oral Reading Miscues: Applied Psycholinguistics*. Newark, DE: International Reading Association.

———. 1996. *On Reading: A Common-Sense Look at the Nature of Language and the Science of Reading*. Portsmouth, NH: Heinemann.

Goodman, Y. 1996. "Revaluing Readers While Readers Revalue Themselves: Retrospective Miscue Analysis." *The Reading Teacher* 49: 600–609.

———. 1997. "Reading Diagnosis: Qualitative or Quantitative?" *The Reading Teacher* 50: 534–538.

Goodman, Y., and A. Marek. 1996. *Retrospective Miscue Analysis: Revaluing Readers and Reading*. Katonah, NY: Richard C. Owen.

Graves, D. 1983. *Writing: Teachers and Children at Work*. Portsmouth, NH: Heinemann.

Green, M. 1998. "Rapid Retrieval of Information: Reading Aloud with a Purpose." *Journal of Adolescent and Adult Literacy* 41: 306–307.

Greene, F. 1979. "Radio Reading." In *Reading Comprehension at Four Linguistic Levels*, ed. C. Pennock. Newark, DE: International Reading Association.

Harris, T., and R. Hodges, eds. 1995. *The Literacy Dictionary*. Newark, DE: International Reading Association.

Henderson, A. 1988. "Parents Are a School's Best Friend." *Phi Delta Kappan* 70: 148–153.

Hewison, J., and J. Tizard. 1980. "Parental Involvement and Reading Attainment." *British Journal of Educational Psychology* 50: 209–215.

Hoffman, J. 1987. "Rethinking the Role of Oral Reading in Basal Instruction." *Elementary School Journal* 87: 367–373.

Hoffman, J., and K. Segel. 1982. Oral Reading Instruction: A Century of Controversy. Paper presented at the annual meeting of the International Reading Association, Anaheim, CA (ERIC Document Reproduction Service No. ED 239 277).

Holdaway, D. 1979. *The Foundations of Literacy*. New York: Ashton-Scholastic.

Huey, E. 1968. *The Psychology and Pedagogy of Reading*. Cambridge, MA: MIT Press.

International Reading Association. 1996. *Standards for the English Language Arts*. Newark, DE: International Reading Association.

Johns, I. 1984. "Students' Perceptions of Reading: Insights from Research and Pedagogical Implications." In *Language Awareness and Learning to Read*. Eds. J. Downing and R. Valtin. New York: Springer-Verlag.

———. 1986. "Students' Perceptions of Reading: Thirty Years of Inquiry." In *Metalinguistic Awareness and Beginning Literacy: Conceptualizing What It Means to Read and Write*. Eds. D. Yaden and S. Templeton. Portsmouth, NH: Heinemann.

Johns, J., and S. Lenski. 1997. *Improving Reading: A Handbook of Strategies*. 2d ed. Dubuque, IA: Kendall/Hunt.

Kobrin, B. 1995. *Eyeopeners II: Children's Books to Answer Children's Questions About the World Around Them*. New York: Scholastic.

Koskinen, P., R. Wilson, L. Gambrell, and S. Neuman. 1993. "Captioned Video and Vocabulary Learning: An Innovative Practice in Literary Instruction." *The Reading Teacher* 47: 36–43.

Long, S., P. Winograd, and C. Bridge. 1989. "The Effects of Reader and Text Characteristics on Reports of Imagery During and After Reading." *Reading Research Quarterly* 24: 353–372.

McCauley, J., and D. McCauley. 1992. "Using Choral Reading to Promote Language Learning for ESL Students." *The Reading Teacher* 45: 526–533.

Miccinati, J. 1985. "Using Prosodic Cues to Teach Oral Reading Fluency." *The Reading Teacher* 39: 206–212.

Morrow, L. 1983. "Home and School Correlates of Early Interest in Literature." *Journal of Educational Research* 76: 221–230, 339–344.

O'Masta, G., and J. Wold. 1991. "Encouraging Independent Reading Through the Reading Millionaires Project." *The Reading Teacher* 44: 656–662.

Opitz, M. 1989. An Investigation of the Importance of Using Student Interviews in the Development of Chapter I Diagnostic Profiles. Unpublished Ph.D. dissertation, University of Oregon.

———. 1995. *Getting the Most from Predictable Books*. New York: Scholastic.

Person, M. 1990. "Say It Right!" *The Reading Teacher* 43: 428–429.

Postlethwaite, T., and K. Ross. 1992. *Effective Schools in Reading: Implications for Educational Planners*. The Hague: International Association for the Evaluation of Educational Achievement.

Pressley, M., P. El-Dinary, I. Gaskins, T. Schuder, J. Bergman, J. Alasi, and R. Brown. 1992. "Direct Explanation Done Well: Transactional Instruction of Reading Comprehension Strategies." *Elementary School Journal* 92: 513–555.

Raphael, T. 1982. "Teaching Question Answer Relationships." *The Reading Teacher* 39: 516–520.

————. 1986. "Question-Answering Strategies for Children." *The Reading Teacher* 36: 186–191.

Rasinski, T. V. 1995. "Fast Start: A Parental Involvement Reading Program for Primary Grade Students." In *Generations of Literacy: The Seventeenth Yearbook of the College Reading Association.* Eds. W. Linek and E. Sturtevant. Harrisonburg, VA: College Reading Association.

Rasinski, T. V., and N. Padak. 1996. *Holistic Reading Strategies: Teaching Children Who Find Reading Difficult.* Englewood Cliffs, NJ: Merrill/Prentice Hall.

Rasinski, T. V., N. Padak, W. Linek, and E. Sturtevant. 1994. "The Effects of Fluency Development Instruction on Urban Second Grade Readers." *Journal of Education Research* 87: 158–164.

Reutzel, D. R., P. Hollingsworth, and J. Eldredge. 1994. "Oral Reading Instruction: The Impact on Student Reading Development." *Reading Research Quarterly* 29: 40–62.

Rhodes, L., and N. Shanklin. 1990. "Miscue Analysis in the Classroom." *The Reading Teacher* 44: 252–254.

Ruddell, R., M. Ruddell, and H. Singer. 1994. *Theoretical Models and Processes of Reading.* 4th ed. Newark, DE: International Reading Association.

Sanacore, J. 1991. "Expository and Narrative Texts: Balancing Young Children's Reading Experiences." *Childhood Education* 67: 211–214.

Savage, J. 1998. *Teaching Reading and Writing: Combining Skills, Strategies, and Literature.* 2d ed. Boston: McGraw-Hill.

Searfoss, L. 1975. "Radio Reading." *The Reading Teacher* 29: 295–296.

Sloan, P., and R. Lotham. 1981. *Teaching Reading Is . . . .* Melbourne: Thomas Nelson.

Smith, Nila Banton. 1925. *One Hundred Ways to Teach Silent Reading, for All Grades.* New York: World Book Company. Out of print

Stanovich, K. 1980. "Toward an Interactive-Compensatory Model of Individual Differences in the Development of Reading Fluency." *Reading Research Quarterly* 16: 32–71.

————. 1986. "Matthew Effects in Reading: Some Consequences of Individual Differences in the Acquisition of Literacy." *Reading Research Quarterly* 21: 360–407.

Strang, R. 1969. *Diagnostic Teaching of Reading.* 2d ed. New York: McGraw-Hill.

Taubenheim, B., and J. Christensen. 1978. "Let's Shoot 'Cock Robin'! Alternatives to 'Round Robin' Reading." *Language Arts* 55: 975–977.

Tompkins, G. 1998. *Fifty Literacy Strategies Step by Step.* Upper Saddle River, NJ: Merrill.

Topping, K. 1987. "Paired Reading: A Powerful Technique for Parent Use." *The Reading Teacher* 40: 608–614.

———. 1989. "Peer Tutoring and Paired Reading: Combining Two Powerful Techniques." *The Reading Teacher* 42: 488–494.

Trelease, J. 1989. *The New Read-Aloud Handbook.* New York: Penguin.

———. 1992. *Hey! Listen to This: Stories to Read Aloud.* New York: Penguin.

Zutell, J., and T. V. Rasinski. 1991. "Training Teachers to Attend to Their Students' Oral Reading Fluency." *Theory into Practice* 30: 211–217.

Children's Literature and Compilations

Aardema, V. 1981. *Bringing the Rain to the Kapiti Plain.* New York: Dial.

Alexander, M. 2003. *I'll Never Share You, Blackboard Bear.* Cambridge, MA: Candlewick.

Alexander, S. H. 2008. *She Touched the World: Laura Bridgman, Deaf-Blind Pioneer.* New York: Clarion.

Allen, K. M. 2003. *The Little Piggy's Book of Manners.* New York: Holt.

Armstrong, J. 1998. *Shipwreck at the Bottom of the World: The Extraordinary True Story of Shackleton and the* Endurance. Read by T. Mali. Middletown, RI: Audio Bookshelf.

Arnosky, J. 2007. *Babies in the Bayou.* New York: G. P. Putnam's Sons.

Arnosky, J. 2008. *The Brook Book: Exploring the Smallest Streams.* New York: Dutton.

Avi. 2008. *A Beginning, a Muddle, and an End: The Right Way to Write Writing.* Orlando, FL: Harcourt.

Ayres, K. 2007. *Up, Down, and Around.* Cambridge, MA: Candlewick.

Babbit, N. 1975. *Tuck Everlasting.* New York: Farrar, Straus & Giroux.

Backes, L. 2001. *Best Books for Kids Who (Think They) Hate to Read: 125 Books That Will Turn Any Child into a Lifelong Reader.* New York: Crown.

Barchers, S. 1997. *Fifty Fabulous Fables: Beginning Readers Theatre.* Westport, CT: Libraries Unlimited.

Barr, C. 2006. *Best Books for Children: Preschool Through Grade 6* (8th ed.). Westport, CT: Libraries Unlimited.

Beaumont, K. 2008. *Who Ate All the Cookie Dough?* New York: Holt.

Belton, S. 2008. *The Tallest Tree.* New York: Greenwillow.

Bentley, J. 1997. *"Dear Friend": Thomas Garrett and William Still.* Brooklyn: Cobblehill Books.

Blackstone, S. 2006. *Walking Through the Jungle.* Cambridge, MA: Barefoot Books.

Blume, J. 1985. *The Pain and the Great One*. New York: Random House Children's Books.

Breen, S. 2007. *Stick*. New York: Dial.

Brown, M. W. 1990. *The Important Book*. New York: HarperCollins.

Bunting, E. 2007. *Hurry! Hurry!* Orlando, FL: Harcourt.

Carle, E. 2001. *Where Are You Going? To See My Friend!* New York: Orchard.

Carter, D. A. 2006. *Woof! Woof!* New York: Little Simon.

Catling, P. 1952. *The Chocolate Touch*. New York: Dell.

Cleary, B. 1981. *Ramona Quimby, Age 8*. New York: HarperCollins.

Cleary, B. 1983. *Dear Mr. Henshaw*. New York: Dell.

Clinton, C. 2007. *When Harriet Met Sojourner*. New York: Amistad.

Collier, J. 1997. *Jazz: An American Saga*. New York: Holt.

Connor, L. 2008. *Waiting for Normal*. New York: Katerine Tegen Books.

Coon, C. F. 2004. *Books to Grow With: A Guide to Using the Best Children's Fiction for Everyday Issues and Tough Challenges*. Portland, OR: Lutra Press.

Corbett, S. 2006. *Free Baseball*. New York: Puffin.

Cotten, C. 2008. *Rain Play*. New York: Holt.

Cronin, D. 2004. *Duck for President*. Read by R. Travis. Norwalk, CT: Weston Woods.

Cummings, P. 2008. *Harvey Moon, Museum Boy*. New York: HarperCollins.

Curlee, L. 2008. *Ballpark: The Story of America's Baseball Fields*. New York: Aladdin.

Cutbill, A. 2006. *The Cow That Laid an Egg*. New York: HarperCollins.

Dahl, R. 1996. *James and the Giant Peach*. New York: Penguin.

DeFelice, C. C. 1997. *Willy's Silly Grandma*. London: Orchard.

DiCamillo, K. 2001. *Because of Winn-Dixie*. Read by C. Jones. Westminster, MD: Listening Library.

Dillon, L. 2007. *Mother Goose, Numbers on the Loose*. Orlando, FL: Harcourt.

Downard, B. 2008. *The Race of the Century*. New York: Simon & Schuster

Draper, S. M. 2006. *Copper Sun*. New York: Simon Pulse.

Dunphy, M. 1996. *Here Is the Wetland*. New York: Hyperion.

Eagle Walking Turtle. 1997. *Eagle Walking Turtle's Full Moon Stories: Thirteen Native American Legends*. New York: Hyperion.

Ehlert, L. 2008. *Oodles of Animals*. Orlando, FL: Harcourt.

Elliott, D. 2008. *On the Farm*. Cambridge, MA: Candlewick.

Falwell, C. 2008. *Scoot!* New York: Greenwillow.

Fleischman, P. 1988. *Joyful Noise*. New York: Harper & Row.

Fleischman, P. 1995. *Bull Run*. New York: HarperCollins.

Fleischman, P. 2008a. *Big Talk, Poems for Four Voices*. Cambridge, MA: Candlewick.

Fleischman, P. 2008b. *The Birthday Tree*. Cambridge, MA: Candlewick.

Fleming, D. 2007. *Beetle Bop*. Orlando, FL: Harcourt.

Floca, B. 2007. *Lightship*. New York: Atheneum.

Florian, D. 2003. *Bow Wow Meow Meow: It's Rhyming Cats and Dogs*. San Diego: Harcourt.

Fox, P. 2008. *Traces*. Asheville, NC: Front Street.

Fradin, J. B. 2002. *Who Was Sacagawea?* New York: Grosset & Dunlap.

Frazee, M. 2003. *Roller Coaster*. San Diego: Harcourt.

Fredericks, A. D. 1993. *Frantic Frogs and Other Frankly Fractured Folktales for Readers Theatre*. Westport, CT: Libraries Unlimited.

Freedman, R. 1994. *Kids at Work*. New York: Clarion.

Funke, C. C. 2005. *Book Sense Best Children's Books: Favorites for All Ages Recommended by Independent Booksellers*. New York: Newmarket.

Gaiman, N. 2004. *The Neil Gaiman Audio Collection.* Read by N. Gaiman. New York: Harper Audio.

Gardiner, J. 1980. *Stone Fox*. New York: Harper & Row.

Garrison, B. 2007. *Only One Neighborhood*. New York: Dutton.

Gerstein, M. 2007. *Leaving the Nest*. New York: Frances Foster Books.

Gibbons, G. 1997a. *Click! A Book About Cameras and Taking Pictures*. New York: Little, Brown.

Gibbons, G. 1997b. *The Honey Makers*. New York: HarperCollins.

Gibbons, G. 2008. *The Planets*. New York: Holiday House.

Gillespie, J. T. 2006. *Best Books for Middle School and Junior High Readers: Supplement to the First Edition: Grades 6–9*. Westport, CT: Libraries Unlimited.

Goldin, B. 1997. *The Girl Who Lived with the Bears*. San Diego: Harcourt.

Goodman, S. 2005. *The Train They Call the City of New Orleans.* Read by T. Chapin. Pine Plains, NY: Live Oak Media.

Gravett, E. 2007. *Monkey and Me*. New York: Simon & Schuster.

Grimes, N. 2008. *Oh, Brother!* New York: Greenwillow.

Halsted, J. W. 2002. *Some of My Best Friends Are Books*. Scottsdale, AZ: Great Potential.

Hamilton, K. 2008. *Red Truck*. New York: Viking.

Hannigan, K. 2004. *Ida B.* Read by L. Taylor. Westminster, MD: Listening Library.

Helakoski, L. 2008. *Big Chickens Fly the Coop*. New York: Dutton.

Herman, C. 2008. *My Chocolate Year*. New York: Simon & Schuster.

Hobbs, W. 1997. *Beardream*. New York: Atheneum.

Hostetter, J. 2008. *Healing Water: A Hawaiian Story*. Honesdale, PA: Calkins Creek.

Hurmence, B. 1997. *Slavery Time: When I Was Chillun*. New York: G. P. Putnam's Sons.

Hurwitz, J. 2002. *Ever-Clever Elisa*. New York: HarperCollins.

Huynh, Q. N. 1999. *Water Buffalo Days*. New York: HarperCollins.

James, S. 1997. *Leon and Bob*. Cambridge, MA: Candlewick.

Janeczko, P. B. 1997. *Home on the Range: Cowboy Poetry*. New York: Dial.

Jarrett, C. 2008. *Arabella Miller's Tiny Caterpillar*. Cambridge, MA: Candlewick.

Jenkins, E. 2004. *My Favorite Thing (According to Alberta)*. New York: Atheneum.

Johnson, A. 1989. *Tell Me a Story, Mama*. New York: Scholastic.

Johnson, A. 2005. *A Sweet Smell of Roses*. New York: Aladdin.

Johnson, A. 2007. *Wind Flyers*. New York: Simon & Schuster.

Johnson, J. W. 2007. *Lift Every Voice and Sing*. New York: Amistad.

Johnston, T. 2003. *Go Track a Yak!* New York: Simon & Schuster.

Kajikawa, K. 2008. *Close to You*. New York: Holt.

Katz, A. 2008. *Oops!* New York: Margaret K. McElderry Books.

Keller, L. 2003. *Arnie the Doughnut*. New York: Holt.

Kipling, R. 1997. *Rikki-Tikki-Tavi*. New York: HarperCollins.

Kirk, D. 2003. *Jack and Jill*. New York: G. P. Putnam's Sons.

Kobrin, B. 1995. *Eyeopeners II: Children's Books to Answer Children's Questions About the World Around Them, K–12*. New York: Scholastic.

Kroll, V. 1997. *Butterfly Boy*. Honesdale, PA: Boyds Mills.

Krosoczka, J. J. 2003. *Bubble Bath Pirates*. New York: Viking.

Krull, K. 1997. *Lives of the Athletes*. San Diego: Harcourt.

Kurtz, J., and C. Kurtz. 1997. *Only a Pigeon*. New York: Simon & Schuster.

Lesesne, T. S. 2003. *Making the Match: The Right Book for the Right Reader at the Right Time, Grades 4–12*. Portland, ME: Stenhouse.

Lewis, P. O. 2003. *The Jupiter Stone*. Berkeley: Tricycle Press.

Littlesugar, A. 1998. *Shake Rag: From the Life of Elvis Presley*. New York: Philomel.

Lobel, A. 1980. *Fables*. New York: HarperCollins.

Lobel, A. 1984. *Days with Frog and Toad*. New York: HarperCollins.

London, J. 2003. *When the Fireflies Come*. New York: Dutton.

Long, M. 2003. *How I Became a Pirate*. Orlando, FL: Harcourt.

Maddox, M. 2008. *A Crossing of Zebras: Animal Packs in Poetry*. Honesdale, PA: Wordsong.

Manushkin, F. 2008. *How Mama Brought the Spring*. New York: Dutton.

McBratney, S. 2005. *One Voice, Please: Favorite Read-Aloud Stories*. Cambridge, MA: Candlewick.

McCarthy, M. 2007. *A Closer Look*. New York: Greenwillow.

McKissack, P., and F. McKissack. 1994. *Black Diamond: The Story of the Negro Baseball Leagues*. New York: Scholastic.

McMullan, K. 2004. *I Stink*. Read by A. Richter. Norwalk, CT: Weston Woods.

McNaughton, C. 1997. *Oops!* San Diego: Harcourt Brace.

Medearis, A. S. 1997. *The Ghost of Sifty-Sifty Sam*. New York: Scholastic.

Meltzer, M. 2008. *Albert Einstein: A Biography*. New York: Holiday House.

Michelson, R. 1996. *Animals That Ought to Be*. New York: Simon & Schuster.

Miranda, A. 1997. *To Market, to Market*. San Diego: Harcourt Brace.

Mora, P. 2002. *This Big Sky*. New York: Scholastic.

Morpurgo, M. 2006. *The Mozart Question*. Cambridge: Candlewick.

Munsch, R. 1997. *Alligator Baby*. New York: Scholastic.

Napoli, D. 2001. *How Hungry Are You?* New York: Atheneum.

Newman, L. 2003. *Pigs, Pigs, Pigs!* New York: Simon & Schuster.

Nolen, J. 2007. *Pitching in for Eubie*. New York: Amistad.

O'Donnell, Elizabeth. 1987. *Maggie Doesn't Want to Move*. New York: Macmillan.

O'Neil, M. 2003. *The Sound of Day, The Sound of Night*. New York: Melanie Kroupa Books.

Olawsky, L. A. 1997. *Colors of Mexico*. New York: First Avenue Editions.

Onyefulu, I. 2006. *Chidi Only Likes Blue*. London: Frances Lincoln Ltd.

Opitz, M. F. 1996. *Getting the Most from Predictable Books*. New York: Scholastic.

Opitz, M. F., and M. P. Ford. 2006. *Books and Beyond: New Ways to Reach Readers*. Portsmouth, NH: Heinemann.

Paterson, K. 2000. *Bridge to Terabithia*. Read by S. P. Leonard. New York: Harper Children's Audio.

Pfeffer, W. 2008. *A New Beginning: Celebrating the Spring Equinox*. New York: Dutton.

Pilkey, D. 1995. *Dragon's Fat Cat*. New York: Scholastic.

Polacco, P. 1994. *Pink and Say*. New York: Philomel.

Potter, J. 1997. *African Americans Who Were First*. Brooklyn: Cobblehill.

Prelutsky, J. 2008a. *My Dog May Be a Genius*. New York: Greenwillow.

Prelutsky, J. 2008b. *Pizza, Pigs, and Poetry: How to Write a Poem*. New York: Greenwillow.

Pringle, L. 2008. *Sharks! Strange and Wonderful*. Honesdale, PA: Boyds Mills.

Purmell, A. 2008. *Maple Syrup Season*. New York: Holiday House.

Rinaldi, A. 2008. *The Redheaded Princess*. New York: HarperCollins.

Robberecht, T. 2007. *Sam Tells Stories*. New York: Clarion.

Rockwell, A. 2008. *President's Day*. New York: HarperCollins.

Root, P. 1997. *The Hungry Monster*. Cambridge, MA: Candlewick.

Root, P. 2008. *One Duck Stuck: A Mucky Duck Counting Book*. Cambridge, MA: Candlewick.

Rylant, C. 1996. *Henry and Mudge Take the Big Test*. New York: Simon & Schuster.

Rylant, C. 2002. *Tulip Sees America*. New York: Scholastic.

Schaefer, L. 2006. *An Island Grows*. New York: Greenwillow.

Schertle, A. 2008. *Little Blue Truck*. Orlando, FL: Harcourt.

Scieszka, J. 2008. *Smash! Crash*. New York: Simon & Schuster.

Sendak, M. 1991. *Chicken Soup with Rice*. New York: HarperTrophy.

Silvey, A. 2005. *100 Best Books for Children: A Parent's Guide to Making the Right Choices for Your Young Reader, Toddler to Preteen*. New York: Houghton Mifflin.

Siy, A. 2008. *One Tractor: A Counting Book*. New York: Holiday House.

Skolsky, M. W. 1999. *Love from Your Friend Hannah*. Read by L. Hamilton. Westminster, MD: Listening Library.

Smith Jr, C. R. 2007. *If: A Father's Advice to His Son*. New York: Atheneum.

Sobol, D. J. 1970. *Encyclopedia Brown Saves the Day*. New York: Puffin.

Spinelli, E. 2003. *Rise the Moon*. New York: Dial.

Spinelli, J. 1992. *Maniac Magee*. New York: Ashton Scholastic.

Stadler, A. 2003. *Lila Bloom*. New York: Frances Foster Books.

Stanley, D. 2008. *The Mysterious Case of the Allbright Academy*. New York: HarperCollins.

Stevens, J. 2003. *Jackalope*. San Diego: Harcourt.

Stevens, J. 2008. *Help Me Mr. Mutt!* Orlando, FL: Harcourt.

Stone, T. L. 2008. *Elizabeth Leads the Way*. New York: Holt.

Tarpley, N. 2003. *I Love My Hair*. New York: Little, Brown.

Thompson, L. 2008. *Wee Little Chick*. New York: Simon & Schuster.

Trelease, J. 2006. *The Read-Aloud Handbook*. New York: Penguin.

Viorst, J. 1984. *If I Were in Charge of the World and Other Worries.* New York: Simon & Schuster.

Wallace, R. 2007. *Winning Season: Curveball*. New York: Puffin.

Watts, I. 2003. *Just a Minute*. San Francisco: Chronicle.

Weatherford, C. B. 2008. *Before John Was a Jazz Giant: A Song of John Coltrane*. New York: Holt.

Weinstein, E. S. 2008. *Everywhere the Cow Says, "Moo!"* Honesdale, PA: Boyds Mills.

Weisburd, S. 2008. *Barefoot: Poems for Naked Feet*. Honesdale, PA: Wordsong.

White, E. B. 1991. *Charlotte's Web*. Read by E. B. White. Westminster, MD: Listening Library.

Willard, E. K. 2008. *Mary Ingalls on Her Own*. New York: HarperCollins.

Winter, J. 2005. *Roberto Clemente: Pride of the Pittsburgh Pirates*. New York: Aladdin.

Wolf, J. M. 2002. *Cinderella Outgrows the Glass Slipper and Other Zany Fractured Fairy Tale Plays*. New York: Scholastic.

Wong, H. Y. 2003. *Tracks In the Snow*. New York: Holt.

Wood, D. 2003. *Old Turtle and the Broken Truth*. New York: Scholastic.

Worthy, J. 2005. *Readers Theatre for Building Fluency*. New York: Scholastic.

Yokota, J. 2001. *Kaleidoscope: A Multicultural Booklist for Grades K–8*. Urbana, IL: National Council of Teachers of English.